REFABULATIONS

ALSO BY SHARON THESEN

Artemis Hates Romance
*Aurora**
The Beginning of the Long Dash
Confabulations: Poems for Malcolm Lowry
The Good Bacteria
Holding the Pose
*News & Smoke: Selected Poems**
Oyama Pink Shale
A Pair of Scissors
The Pangs of Sunday
The Receiver
The Wig-Maker

AS EDITOR

*After Completion: The Later Letters of Charles Olson and Frances
Boldereff** (with Ralph Maud)
Charles Olson and Frances Boldereff: A Modern Correspondence (with
Ralph Maud)
The New Long Poem Anthology
The New Long Poem Anthology (second edition)*
*The Vision Tree: Selected Poems of Phyllis Webb**

* Published by Talonbooks

REFABULATIONS

SELECTED LONGER POEMS

Sharon Thesen

EDITED BY ERÍN MOURE

TALONBOOKS

Talonbooks
9259 Shaughnessy Street, Vancouver, British Columbia, Canada v6p 6r4
talonbooks.com

Talonbooks is located on xʷməθkʷəy̓əm, Sḵwx̱wú7mesh, and səlilwətaʔɬ Lands.

First printing: 2023

Typeset in Arno
Printed and bound in Canada on 100% post-consumer recycled paper

Interior and cover design by Typesmith
Cover artwork: #11 from solo exhibit *Targeting Light Sources*, 2009
acrylics and graphite on wood, 24 × 48 in. by Marion Llewellyn

Talonbooks acknowledges the financial support of the Canada Council for the
Arts, the Government of Canada through the Canada Book Fund, and the Province
of British Columbia through the British Columbia Arts Council and the Book
Publishing Tax Credit.

Library and Archives Canada Cataloguing in Publication

Title: Refabulations : selected longer poems / Sharon Thesen, edited by Erín Moure.
Other titles: Poems. Selections
Names: Thesen, Sharon, -1946 author. | Moure, Erín, -1955 editor.
Description: Includes bibliographical references and index.
Identifiers: Canadiana 20220481962 | ISBN 9781772015102 (softcover)

Classification: LCC PS8589.H433 A6 2023 | DDC C811/.54—dc23

For Robin Blaser (1925–2009)

poet, teacher, friend

Resuscitate the form out of the line ...
exorcise the shadows.
   —Etel Adnan
    Journey to Mount Tamalpais

Contents

xiii   Sharon Thesen: Renegade *Refabulator* of the Everyday
(Erín Moure)

3   Interspersal 1: After Roy Kiyooka's Funeral

7   Five Preludes
12   A Pair of Scissors

31   Interspersal 2: Biography of a Woman

35   The Beginning of the Long Dash
49   Six
55   Being Adults

61   Interspersal 3: The Watermelon

65   The Occasions
69   Gala Roses
79   From Toledo

85   Interspersal 4: Clematis Montana Rubens

89   Parts of Speech
99   I Drive the Car

103   Interspersal 5: The Parrot

107   Confabulations

139   Interspersal 6: Skylarks

143   The Fire
154   The Good Bacteria

169   Interspersal 7: The Celebration

173   Weeping Willow
184   Radio New France Radio

197   Interspersal 8: Oh, Hello Count, How Are You, Do Come In

201   A Holy Experiment
206   The Nets of Being
217   The Consumptives at Tranquille Sanatorium, 1953
223   At My Mother's in Prince George

231   Interspersal 9: In the Car Wash

233   Care for the Plenitude of the World (Sharon Thesen)

239   Acknowledgments
240   Notes
242   List of Original Publications
243   Selected Bibliography
246   Index of First Lines and Titles

Re
fab
ula
tions

Sharon Thesen

Renegade *Refabulator* of the Everyday

Sharon Thesen is a poet who has surprised me and given me joy
and wry laughter for over forty years, renewing my belief in the
poem, renewing my need for poetry, ever since I first discov-
ered her work in 1980, in a used bookstore on West Broadway in
Vancouver, in *Artemis Hates Romance*.

Her work in the long poem, the serial poem – both her own
repertoire and the works of others that she twice edited into the
most beautiful of anthologies[1] – is legendary among poets of
my generation. Thesen makes of the poem a space of thinking,
of questioning, where deft thrusts of self-deprecatory humour
prickle up alongside metapoetic observation which, in turn,
surges up not from any theory but from the materiality and
rhythms of dailiness – cooking for birthdays, driving the car, the
dog's romp, a haircut, a time signal, the natural world or what we
call nature – in an ongoingness and an insistence on attention that
Thesen has called, in a typical quip, her "aggressive poignancy."
Hers is a cascade of language that trips and rights, moves, then
stands still looking out at the sky, because why not, because there
it is, look! We're tiny beings, and so lucky.

Sharon Thesen is a renegade of the everyday, of the image, of
tone and balance and of tipping that balance, too, only to regain
it again, on a different level, as if we'd just stepped off an escalator
onto a new floor. She's a renegade but a poet of community, too.
And she is a renegade *in* the poetry community, inside the flow of

---

1   *The New Long Poem Anthology*, see bibliography.

what is produced, insisted upon, turned into "schools" of thought. Towards such schools of thought she is a contrarian, even as she is insistent on thinking. Like the Galician early-modernist poems of Rosalía de Castro (impossible to find an antecedent in English), her poems have an almost "sly" *retranca* at times, a wit that pokes its elbow at irony, without being "ironic." She's a feminist against making fixities of feminism, a thinker in the poem who resists those who have theories and for whom thinking is a device that speaks *at* us, to find us wanting or to absolve us. Thesen's work speaks *among* us; in reading her, we neighbour her, and she gives us a neighbourhood.

Her work is a restless geopoetry of British Columbia. It is inhabited by the natural world, by long-time friends, her son, her parents, poets and writers she has read. Present, too, are glints of settler histories that have etched traces and carried Thesen from place to Western place: Old Massett (G̲aw Tlagée) on Haida Gwaii, Kamloops of the Tranquille Sanatorium, Prince George, Vancouver, Oyama in the Okanagan interior valley of the Syilx Okanagan People. Yet her poetry is not autobiographical. It is sited. The "I," in its role as speaking position, while constantly and restlessly in the process of formulating Sharon Thesen and indexing others, allows images to open the reader to the huge world of "the poem," in which small things happen, "take place," show us up, and provoke wonder in us: laughter, resistance, and calm. Thesen is a renegade, a refabulator, a renegade refabulator at work in the poem.

She's long been a poet who enacts a human relation to a natural world, nurturing what today we'd call an ecopoetics. But she doesn't need this name any more than she needs any other. When Garry Thomas Morse at Sage Hill Writing asked her in 2015 about her relation to landscape and Gary Snyder's conception of "the wild," Thesen responded:

> I honestly don't think you can even sensibly talk about the role or influence of landscape on writing, since it seems to be endemic to or substantially present in every perception

or feeling or image we have. Landscape and narrative. We are born into, and exist in, "an actual earth of value" (to use Olson's phrase) that is geographical, spiritual, and linguistic all at the same time.

Earlier, to Daphne Marlatt in the *Capilano Review*, she quoted Snyder more fully, reminding us that he links "wild" to "mind." For Thesen, this evokes mental health:

> Sanity is a rare and under-appreciated condition, usually and mistakenly allied with repression. Whereas I believe sanity is the social and psychological equivalent of what Snyder calls "the wild": as Snyder says, "interconnected, interdependent, incredibly complex. Diverse, ancient, and full of information." Snyder says a poem is a "creature of the wild mind." By "wild" and "sane" I mean elegant, complex, subtle, and clear as a bell even as it must muddy the waters of the given.

Perhaps those waters of the given are muddy because we're beings of earth, not water. Sharon Thesen situates herself in poetry, in a sense, between foreshore and *barranco*, between a place full of shells that teems with life and food, and the pit, the abyss, the earth where we die, where wolves are, where shadows lie deep. If she doesn't believe in the (urban and white-settler) notion of rewilding, she does believe in paying attention, and her attention is wild and unruly. For Thesen, we are always situated within *land*-scape, and within *land* (landscape is always something portrayed; land is something inhabited or "seen" by the speaker as inhabited), and we are always a "we."

Thesen's images are of the world she lives in, of that reality that she/we make/s in perceiving; they are not confession. They are "about" something, as she says, calling herself a poet of "aboutism." The poems explore, reflect, refract, laugh, and press on the gas pedal, turn left though the light is yellow and it's raining, then pull into the parking space so the author can dash out after food or flowers, pulling the reader with her into the streets and the world. Yet they are still linguistic acts: she uses "&" and "and" differently, for different sounds and liaisons, for example. She considers the spaces between stanzas and parts of a serial poem with attention: each time the listening uncovers, perhaps, a variation in form. Then, too, the voice of the poems springs up and the poem can mention itself, mention the poem, and invoke the writers of history, for all poems are also "about" language, about history, about we who are constantly situating ourselves in relation to others.

In poems such as "The Fire," she sees – and this, twenty years ago – the effects of settlement on a changing BC climate, and the changing climate's return effect on settlement (now no surprise), a mutuality that calls for urgent change and an end to innocence.

"The Beginning of the Long Dash" is classic Thesen. She takes us to a quintessentially Canadian moment, especially for Canadians raised with the radio on, its needle on the national public station: the beginning of a long noise following ten seconds of silence. She makes us stop and consider what time really means: in a polity, in a country, in a life buffeted by other lives. The noise that follows silence: what relation does that noise have with silence, and does that relation really tell us anything about time? Her poem unfolds *at the beginning* of the long dash; it is not the long dash or the silence. From that beginning, Thesen releases a symphonic sequence of images of dailiness, in THIS country, in a kind of flow, a cascade or soundscape, a murmur that nourishes and constructs us (us, too, as readers!). Interspersed amid the images are metapoetical, metalinguistic thoughts or formulations – sparks – that spring not from theories but from the images themselves. With these thoughts, these sparks, we are renewed in our own readerly production/creation/reception of images, and it is we as readers receiving these images and insights who complete the poem. The poem is an acute juxtaposition of ordinary seeing, its precision, in the "seek" of language in a world where even the mundane is astonishing: where (wryly) "*sex, free, cure, money,* and *baldness*" are the "five most compelling words" in the language.

Thesen is also adept in minimalist line forms, taking us in "Six," "Being Adults," and "Parts of Speech" through a short-line density that opens the page, the poem proceeding serially so that each piece generates the next, is its seed. Seriality is no ordinary narrative progression; it involves language generating language, so that "narrative" does not continue in the usual way. Some might call its effects "disjunctive," but it is really a different mode of junction.

"Gala Roses" is different in form; long-lined, single-line stanzas (a homage to New Zealand poet Michele Leggott, Thesen's contemporary) bring a different kind of attention to bear on the image, and on the images' unfolding. Thesen's use of such different forms in the serial and longer poem stems from her attentiveness to the rhythms and pacing of description, of thought (and within her forms there is, of course, even more variety, change-up, and a sense of play). Always, in Thesen's work, form follows function. This is consistent with work in the serial poem, which functions not by following a preset form or progression but by leading into and propelling a shape in an ongoingness, a movement, restless and resistant. And by "function," I mean the verb, not the noun! In some languages and cultures, nouns *are* verbal, are stills of what is ever and always in motion, and it seems to me that Sharon Thesen belongs (without knowing it) to those languages.

Thesen's poems never stand still. They confabulate, fabulate, and refabulate. Before we close the back cover of *Refabulations*, the poem's voice emerges in its vehicle from the car wash, after receiving a wet whooshing and very noisy buffeting during a read of the monk Thomas Merton writing on "silence." Here is the poem making the poem, buffing the poem, and emerging with its poet to brush past weeds and branches in a laneway: the urban wild, the minimal, the breakthrough. The poem "In the Car Wash" is to me an allegory for the writing and revising of a poem, a book.

In *Refabulations*, the poems burst from prior layers of text and interrogation, from years of poetic practice, to be created and recreated *here*. They are brought into new context, and this generates new reverberations and meanings. To recontextualize out of chronological order, to put one poem beside another poem from another book and era: this is a generative gesture.

Refabulations is above all a book created by a self-professed "receiver," a poet who was a lover of poetry even as a child, and who in university leaped into literary study. She worked then as a typist of poetry, of interviews, for other poets – her (male, back then) professors. To the flora and fauna of the foreshores of British Columbia and of its interiors, to its climates, to her life as a woman, our intrepid typist added literary knowledges. In her work, the depth of these knowledges is never far: glints of Coleridge, of Malcolm Lowry – a writer figure who melds the Old World of England with the New of BC and Mexico – of H.D., of Virginia Woolf transported to the southeast British Columbia woods. Hemingway appears, Olson, Mozart, Pope. We hear many echoes of Berkeley Renaissance poet Jack Spicer (whom she studied, via Robin Blaser) and Phyllis Webb (whose work she edited, bringing the amplitude of Webb's vital practice into our full purview in the early 1980s). Frances Boldereff is an enduring guide and traveller, as is Dogfish Woman, long an inspiring figure for Thesen. And Roy Kiyooka is alive in the book's invocation, its first poem. We write, because we must, in the presence of our forebears.

But why poetry? Why did our receiver persist with poetry? Why does her work persist and engage us years after it was written? I think Sharon Thesen herself puts a finger on an answer, in an online poetics statement at *Poetry in Canada*, when she says:

Poetic form allows me to appreciate "the magic of persons" (a term Robin Blaser used) and the magic of situations all at once. Poetry is more like nature – some would say wild nature – than civilization. This is something I derive from my abiding interest in the Romantic poets – Coleridge, Blake, Shelley, Clare, Keats. You can walk around naked in a poem, you can converse with whales and other, sometimes dead, poets, and weep over the death of a mouse. You can let other people say what they want and need to say, for themselves.

Again, community teems here: the poets of the historical moment, and the animals, and the friends and neighbours in the poem's continual present.

Knowing that most of Thesen's books had gone out of print and her work in the longer and serial poem was thus not accessible to new generations of readers, I hatched a plan, out of an adamant dream. I challenged Sharon Thesen to take up once again her first, early role as typist and type up anew – for she has never kept current with Word or technology and has no digital copies of her old manuscripts – a sweeping selection of her own work, taking the material result of her lifelong practice of attention and language and recreating it through her own fingers, turning the vibration of letters and computer and the brightness of the screen into a new book for a new generation of readers.

In the process of carrying out the task, Thesen could, if she liked, cut or alter, refabulate the poems she was typing, see what her fingers would urge her to do. And she agreed, and it happened. I came up with a possible table of contents; we discussed it, altered it, ate sushi and tiny bits of squid at "the office" in Kelowna, added poems, crossed some out, then showed our list to Catriona Strang at Talonbooks, who gave us a green light. When Thesen set to typing, I watched what she was up to on Google Docs (Thesen TV!), making notes, then when she was finished, I added back in chunks of what she'd cut (horrors! she cut too much!). On reflection, she replaced some poems with others, and we discussed, and a few more poems simply absconded, and a few others took off their coats and settled in.

The result, *Refabulations*, includes most of what Thesen wishes to assemble and reactivate of her "longer" poems: serial works, sequences, long takes published between 1980 and 2016.

With them, between them, are interspersed selected nodes of shorter poems. It seems to me that these poems belong with their friends in the book, for Thesen writes single poems with the same breath expansion that propels her longer poems. They read as if windows onto a longer poem, onto the unwritten, and as if they come from the same serial impetus: to be "about" a world and open up its intersections, glows, insistences in the life of a woman trying to figure it all out (and in the process, they often give a good bump to the reader's funny bone).

Thesen's world is urban, yes, but touched by land and earth in a way that belies her growing up in a time in which urban and rural were much more intercalated than they are today (although with climate change, this split is becoming less viable as a way to think of the earth; the wild of the rural is present everywhere). Hers is not a writing that is turned towards the past, however, for today, more than ever, each tiny bit of land and plant and ecology needs care and consideration if we humans are to survive and continue without a great extinction levelling us (for the earth will win out). Thesen's work remains current, vital: it traces the daily effort of attention and *partage* that maintains human sanity in and among the wreckage. Thesen's tactic is one of Rilkean praise at all times: No plant is a weed! No dog is homely!

And none of it, Sharon Thesen admits, is easy, and this is important to recognize. At times it seems she's dancing lightly in her poems, but each one is the result of a labour, and conscience, but also a self-criticism, a thinking that does not want to fall into woe. From her poetics statement at *Poetry in Canada*:

> I struggle with the poem, it struggles with me. I don't find
> writing poetry easy, it's just that poetry is the place where I
> can leave the pressure of normative discourse behind – or try
> to. It's not to make admirable statements but a place to be free
> and alive, to discover things, that is, the profound and usually
> hidden connections between and among things in the world,
> in time, in space, in language. For me, poetry and life are the
> same urge – that is, real life, which is so large that it is hidden

until you start writing the poem and then more and more of it is revealed. My general belief is what Charles Olson wrote in his essay "Human Universe": "Art is the only twin life has, its only valid metaphysic."

Art is life's twin, I like that. And Sharon Thesen is receiver of both art and life, so as to share them with you, readers. You can take this book off the shelf and bring it to the cashier; I hope the sun is streaming into the bookstore through a break in the clouds, as it was for me over forty years ago when I held my own first Thesen book in my hands. *Refabulations* is yours now!

—ERÍN MOURE
MONTRÉAL, MAY 28, 2022

WORKS CITED

Thesen, Sharon. "Get to Know the Poet." Poetry in Canada. Accessed July 2022. www.poetrycanada.org/digital-library-archive/sharon-thesen#Sharon ThesenGettoKnow.

——. "An Interview with Sharon Thesen." By Garry Thomas Morse. Sage Hill Writing. Accessed July 2022. web.archive.org/web/20141031171929/www .sagehillwriting.ca/an-interview-with-sharon-thesen.

——. "'masquerading as simple description': A Conversation with Sharon Thesen." By Daphne Marlatt. *The Capilano Review* 3, no. 5 (Spring 2008). thecapilanoreview.com/interview-with-sharon-thesen/.

——. "Poetics Statement." Poetry in Canada. Accessed July 2022. www.poetrycan ada.org/digital-library-archive/sharon-thesen#SharonThesenStatement.

Interspersal 1

AFTER ROY KIYOOKA'S FUNERAL

I take a kitchen chair out to the front porch
and stand on it to reach the light.
Encased in amber bubbled
glass, which has to be unscrewed
in three small places. The screws are brass,
stiff, unused to suffering. Then the
40-watt bulb comes out and in goes
a 100-watt bulb. The amber casing
back on, with its old cheap bracing
screws. Now
my visitors. Now the path
is lit farther out – and
the way in brighter,
bigger.

Five Preludes

A Pair of Scissors

What's your love? she might say to him. And she knew his answer; how it is the most important thing in the world and no woman possibly understood it. Very well. But could any man understand what she meant either? about life?

—Virginia Woolf, *Mrs Dalloway*

FIVE PRELUDES

1.

Someone about to go back to the hotel room
was thinking about her hat, actually,
two hats. She would put on
the grey hat or the green hat.
She was a different person in the green hat,
more open-minded. Not a hummingbird
green but a black green like the North Shore.
In the grey hat she had less patience
and a stone sat between her legs.
She could already see herself putting
the blue card in the door handle, the green
light flash once. She would reach into the
closet shelf where the hats lay side by side
like those who died for Truth and Beauty in
Dickinson's poem & choose one in *agnosia*,
in darkness, and descend to the town's
winter sales past the cemetery greyly
gleaming in *Phoebus's* gentle rays.

2.

Someone about to climb a hill
decides to take the animals' path
instead of the beaten track
but soon it takes certain dark turns
amid crowding trees below radioactive
cliffs of Oyama pink shale & seems to narrow
and grow vague, vague as the perorations of
greybeards like herself in the academies of Yes
and of Total Access, she herself an open door
but more, the light it sheds across the carpeting
a parallelogram containing the shade of W.B. Yeats
whom Ireland couldn't contain, nor the weather.
What have we now but a wall of younger granite, slate-blue
& crumbling like the ziggurats of yore, and is this
battened-down place in the bunchgrass the animals'
bedroom? Breathless now, her green hat folded in her pocket
she backs down and away, as if condemned at the docket.

3.

Someone about to go to an event
was wondering if she should have some pistachios first or wait.
If she waited, she might keel over and then what.
The evening would bore on like an auger drill
that digs into heartwood & sends up spirals of fragrant
beige curls. While standing in her boudoir
Flight 246 passed overhead & her socks
left crimps in the flesh of her ankles betraying
last-minute preparations as she crosses naked shins
in the armchair of absentia, of the lamentations
catalogued in the catalogue of Malcolm Lowry's personal effects:
charred manuscripts and a photograph of an old ginger cat.
Buckles up her sandals like a Greek bust with tidy coif,
a spray of Mitsouko and then they're off.

4.

Someone about to make a tomato sandwich
opens the fridge door and reckons the laden racks,
the many jars and misty tubs
below, caress of parsley, smear of red pepper
like a goldfish, the *poisson rouge*
of Matisse's paintings in which three to five
dwell in a glass bowl beside an
odalisque reading a novel or writing a letter.
Dear Malcolm, it says, *I shall never forget*
the afternoon we spent on the mudflats
picking up kelp & seashells in our bathing suits.
I beg you, be careful! The fish flit, blips
of orange hue, transparent fins undulant
& aloft, beautiful things,
and all of them – fish, Malcolm, odalisque –
far away from the Roundup
and technologies courtesy of Krupp.

5.

Someone about to be thrown out the door by Ernest Hemingway
adjusts his hat, later to apologize by special
delivery. Not a brighter sun could infuse the world
with blueness and whiteness than the one that lit
this palm-tree-shaded event. She came across it on Wikipedia,
consternation deepening the lines inscribed in her cheeks &
radiating from the corners of her orbs like the gills of Dogfish Woman
resurrected from under the grey seas of Haida Gwaii
– this shocking event in the "quiet, uneventful life" of Wallace Stevens.
Such a fracas could lead a person permanently astray, throw him
out the window of time and space, like the esemplastic power of the
imagination which was ignited in Stevens by the first sightings,
on a regular basis, of the Florida Keys,
which could just about send him to his knees.

A PAIR OF SCISSORS

1.

To be bold in my own way,

to pour myself into something
I can stand & would stand all day

as long as the uniform were some
Yohji Yamamoto thing that didn't cost too much

and the city gave me something back.

2.

Those known as Romani are never too busy
or too stupid to waste an emotion
in spite of persecution and poverty according
to *Latcho Drom.*

Suit jackets worn in the back of a truck,
violins, head scarves, happy babies
passed around, vodka, and funerals –
they know how to live!

3.

What am I doing here? A gasp
of milky starlight through last night's window,
raggy butterflies in daylight rise and sink
& also pieces of tree fluff on the wind
blowing in from the lake. Describe it, too:

choppy today, whitecaps in the binoculars

Morning was grey and cool, cobweb. We walked
to one neighbour's to make a phone call
another's to plug in the hair dryer

Mr. Walsh passing the machine down my tresses
along the path of the puffy brush, lake breeze
finishing the job on the way back through the woods.

4.

"I just go with the flow," says Mr. Walsh,
the blow-dryer the sigh of the soul
in a soulless world,
the sentence
that precedes "Religion is the opium
of the people." And opiates are the mice
of time, especially
mice brought up with a wire mother
not a soft mother. Wiry
were my own limbs though
adoring and strong in the sweet
sad photos of that time, with the baby,
the atrocious marriage, my wedding band
lost in the sea off Kits Beach
in broad daylight, I must have willed it off –

"Me, I just go with the flow," says Mr. Walsh,
snipping at my bangs. Human hair
is deer repellent if spread round the garden,
piles of it came out like a horrid grave
from the compost one day I was
planting roses, repelled, thick hanks of blond
and brown hair, Mr. Walsh recycling.

Like an old terrified ballad, deer freeze
then propel themselves up the hill encumbered
by antlers, twin children, and with knees like horses.

5.

Someone had stepped on my glasses, strangers
were somehow not strangers, everyone got drunk,
two deck chairs were fused in the snow. This
was the dream. It takes me a long time to move into
what's real.

6.

The rain might pass over as a certain breeze
just brushing up the sides of the poplars
lifting the leaves over silvery side up,
& do us a favour the day of the party.

Mrs. Dalloway mends her green dress
surprised by the past and its ever-present infernal
penknife, insistently satisfied with things, &
nervous in the presence of the beloved.

Choosing blossoms at the florist's
while ambulances clang by:

Amethyst dahlias, yellow zinnias, coral tiger lilies.

Late summer season of the king.

My cake last night came out a flop but
crowned with jaunty candles makes the cutest jester cap.

7.

Lightning bolts of silver, lead, zinc
announced by white boulders so many they
look like cows on a farm, resting.

Mr. Walsh a fiend with a pickaxe
pulling granite stones out of the earth
his stiff silver hair
spraying like rays of a hot moon.

The anguished whispered voice of Mrs. Dalloway
in the dark beside the house, "you want
too much!" or something to that effect –
it's hard to hear her in the din of the creek
water and stone piling down from nowhere
in a hurry to find the lake, another life
in clouds

While old free-spirited friends
now propertied and fat open
an invitation, mark on the calendar space
of August 23 "birthday party – bring guacamole."

8.

Fat bees nestle in the oregano patch
going madly to seed in a purple haze

Cabbage moths bounce the air, dragonflies
zoom in, their faces like radios

Opal booty of sky and water, the old ghost
miner who pinches my bum when I step
into the bathtub outside relays from the trees
the coordinates on his compass

Bears strain the last berry bushes
for a mouthful before the snow

A blue velvet prince the Steller's jay
helps himself to fall ryegrass newly planted in beds
that look like the graves of tall persons
laid head to foot

The boat of their souls gently unmoored
amid a white smoke of sighs
in some billionth galaxy by a bending,
untying constellation.

9.

Nearly naked elfin man working on the roof.
Hammer pounds down. Cracks in the heat.

My glaring green dress takes its place
in a village full of brave unhappy women, you'd think
it was medieval Russia, or the future

As in Doris Lessing's *The Memoirs of a Survivor*
& the jaded women of a dead civilization
for whom love is no gateway
but a bitter detour
leading away from life, from purposes

The dress slightly mended, a cuff taken up
with a few tiny stitches

The men do all right, they marry again,
start another family, their old wives
in the garden with primrose and goldenseal,
vinegar remedies and love potions for the bathtub

Mrs. Dalloway dons a bikini and shivers into the
huge blue lake, Mr. Walsh on the beach behind her.

At 52, Mrs. Dalloway has flowers and a menu
to choose, a guest list and seating plan.

Immersed in heavy coldness, the legs
of Mrs. Dalloway pump and waver,
waver and pump, doing the frog kick.

10.

Too early for red wine too late for coffee
Too late to figure out what to do
Too early to really worry about it

Whatever it is seems to duck and waver,
a candle flame when the windows are open & the strafed
nights of August are blooming

Conversation
elliptical, distracted,
going nowhere, could

In the presence
of Mr. Walsh's nervous penknife rip it
apart, her life, and expose

A woman placing on the mantelpiece
a crystal leaping dolphin just so.

11.

New movement in the woods
as autumn paints her russet
shades and yellowy gradually
the odd leaf twirls down
in a rhythm of surprises

& the squirrel runs around
busy with little hands poking

still a bee here & there
still a daisy or two

veins of ore below still frozen
in terror by the conflagration

that ensued when *Phoebus's* reckless son
panicked at the reins of the solar chariot,
drove in too close and charred
this edge of the world.

12.

On the sofa, the cat and a nickel. She
leaves dead moles white belly up
on the path, they having ceased
to entertain her. In the woods
the sawed-off limbs of cedar lie
fragrant on black humus oozing spring water,
and the view beyond is amazing.

The booming cold blue lake goes deep
as the high mountains above,
crowned with surprised wildflowers clutched
in the right hand of Persephone
newly wed in hell.

As for me I did not think up
a new invention, start my own company
on funds borrowed, begged, and stolen,
work twelve hours a day seven days a week
and now have two hundred and fifty employees, no

I am in a charred yellow bathtub
in the forest with Mr. Walsh,
smoke wafting from the fire underneath,
our heads crowned with wreaths of willow & thyme, bound
to that chapter of alchemy

solutio, the dissolution.

13.

The shadow of Mr. Walsh
cuts the shadow of
my hair on the ground beside us

like an old play acted in front of a sheet

in a small forgotten town some travelling

troupe puts on, old hands
at rising to occasions

and also with farces. Finished
with me he shakes out my bib and says
my hair looks great but to myself
I look like a biker and would rather

be a Leo like
Jackie Kennedy – perfection
on horseback & when whispering at banquets

And when she had to be Proserpina
She was not happy. Her face was pinched with fear.
Nevertheless, she was a great queen.

14.

Sick of language,
would rather be an animal
chewing on the side of the road

run away when scared

not just change the subject
sublimate, think up

words with and worth
a spring-coloured daffodil, or jonquil
coloured quarter moon

peeping like a child
over the rim of its crib
clambering to palm-sized feet

when the Earth was young and humanless
and veins of ore were cooling
under Mr. Walsh's vegetable garden

barrows of bark mulch dumped on the pathways
between the beds black and grave
awaiting seed, bird, bee, worm

through cold nights and chill mornings
soaked with dew roses drink the last of
blooming madly like people one hour
into happy hour

Mrs. Dalloway admires the decanted claret
but even more its crystal urn

as for the dead youth she wept considering
love and despair her crystal tear.

15.

After considering the death by suicide
of the young man deranged by war the ambulance
made such a noise about

After the departure of the last guests
Mrs. Dalloway removes her green dress
her shoes, her underthings, her jewellery

The lines scored by the penknife of regret
on the removed eroticism of her body

Despite the three-times daily ingestion
of Ambrotose Plus Vegetable and Herbal Extract –
"Manna from Heaven."

16.

Mr. Walsh has placed a mirror on top of
the shed to attract his friend the raven:
"Black Beauty," he calls to the sky, "I have
something here for you" –
He blows a whistle
and says, "Caw Caw" – "Come on down"

We'd gotten up early to do the dishes, blow
the smoke out of our hair

Someone's hat on a windowsill,
a pink raku bowl mysterious in a paper bag by the stairs,
bouquets of yellow and maroon zinnias, white gladioli,
trout bones laid aside on a plate

Dave Smith left a nearly full bottle of tequila
on the kitchen counter & the Temptations were
still whizzing around in the CD player.

17.

Plump bees nestle in the oregano patch, it's all
going to seed out there, we toil like rescue workers
with shovel and hoe, free a tiny garlic clove here
tiny potato there like forgotten runt children
in the orphanage of underground

A crowd of ten-foot-high
purple dahlias struck down and dug up, massive tubers
heavy under the ground

Sweeping the floor, someone singing
Spanish on the radio

Small headache, two cups of coffee –

Everyone had a wonderful time –

Everyone took home an armload of dahlias,
dark purple with mustard yellow centres
each head round and lovely in the night –

The flashlight beams of everyone
braiding down the road.

Interspersal 2

BIOGRAPHY OF A WOMAN

She was so intelligent
she could see wind and hear
the coughing of flies,
in the basement she worried
about things that hadn't happened yet
but could, her suitors
were swans or had an arm
missing, she lost their engagement
rings, their car keys, was beaten,
shunned, kidnapped, she woke
in a deep well, fled & was captured,
forced to sort through ten tons
of rhillet, pearl rice, popcorn seeds
all night by haughty types who
tortured her with impunity, jealous
of her hair, her goodness that led
to betrothal and them snarky &
evil behind the curtain
as she stepped into the golden
crystal carriage but then she lost
the keys or spilled the wax or
dropped the stitch or found
a dwarf – was dropped off
in the woods at night & forced to sew
starlight into shirts enough
for an army, had her hands chopped off,
her feet removed, was mistaken for a broom
& left in a corner, she had to clean up
after devils and soldiers –
she was so intelligent she
was the chosen bride of the king's son
because she was so beautifully starved
that apples flung themselves off apple trees
into her grown-back hands at midnight.

The Beginning of the Long Dash

———

Six

———

Being Adults

THE BEGINNING OF THE LONG DASH

❋

In the Fashion Tress beauty salon
the Christmas tree is covered with white ornaments,
angels twirl from the ceiling, a quiet crèche
in the alcove beyond the row
of pink hairdryers & old women
dozing beneath them or reading about Fergie
in *Hello!* magazine. Cotton-batten
snow contains miniature lights, a miniature
dog with a ribbon in its ponytail scrabbles
and barks at the window –
until the cash register
marks eviction and pain, the grey raining street
and shoppers burdened with menus and occasions,
the obligations of merriment.
But this is the truth.
The five most compelling words
are *sex, free, cure, money,* and *baldness,*
a chain of conditions ranging from heaven to hell
& soul in the shed like a jar of canned heat.
What does the body of the polar bear
inscribe upon her winter residence, months on end
in the dark? Scraping the ice away
in her sleep –

the goddess language
stretches among the remains
of the forest & the world closes around her
seamless and blue as the ocean
glimpsed from a long way off.
Now we've discovered the true newness
of the broken world
of discourse, our own being finds a place
& mode of expression, not a New World post-colonized
beach where Pocahontas
disports herself doing cartwheels. Fierce
bees assault our summer days
like mass hallucinations of war planes
& when the text says jump
we say How high? The moon winks,
closes her jaundiced eye,
her lockjaw & salacious grin.

❄ ❄

Life awaits us
just around the corner
from the nasty demon in the woods
whose sanctimonious explanations
for the necessity of violence
are daily nightmares of the news.
The various cadres try to reply
above it all, & so
below, so *here* the workers will
drop their shuttles, loom and weave
coming around the corner from the office party.
The party of the particular.
She is very particular
about the arrangement of things
on the coffee table,

the stack of art books
full of beauty, often formula,
their cost sometimes in the three figures.
This vase, that candle.
A still life with silverware,
gaping exposed oysters
sliced lemons, the dead grouse.
There's nothing to eat
but images to hunger for
and how vast & impending the space
occupied by beauty! However
just the slightest thing off
& it refuses to enter, shy inamorata,
to cohabit with the real, a fusion
of atomistic signs resisting
the atavistic pull
back
into the slop of felt life.
Consider that we evolve
only as we return & exchange places
with the muted and the silent
and translate the cries, the surging grief.
No one is immune from the condition
of abuse, the animals ring us
in our sleep, the remains of the forest
crackling like flags in the zeitgeist.

❋ ❋ ❋

What being awaits us
in the land of soldiers
whose flesh alone is uniform
minus the smart reds, blues,
blacks, and brasses of their buttons,
their chinstrap headgear and precise

armament. High on Mont Blanc
she dreams of her lover far away,
a soldier, & inhales the scent
of alpine flowers, a goat
bleating in the distance.
This is beautiful & the topic
of myriad songs, all of which end
on a hopeful note.
Reseeing is what we long for in absence,
from a height so great
the world is simply pattern below us,
pleasing enough. *Au revoir*
echoing among the mountaintops
in the chill wind that gathers
and floats the balloons of our thoughts.
Some are helium, some merely CO_2. *Bios*
the only fit topic of speech,
not speech itself but the field of it.
Discourse worlds itself
in the remains of the forest
& the weeping of children & animals
we don't want to hear. Not show business,
not career.

❀ ❀ ❀ ❀

Upon what stretch of the imagination
do we imagine ourselves stranded.
Kublai Khan, Corpus Christi,
West Edmonton Mall, some canoe
on some poor river clogged
with blood and grease from the nearby
slaughterhouse. Beneath the intersections
of windy Canadian cities
howling with winter the citizens

wander, wondering among display racks,
ghostly & washed up
as Elpenor in joyless regions.
I try on clothes,
pose in sunglasses,
keep out from under the thinning ozone.
An eight-by-ten manila envelope
lies on the coffee table
with the art books, the other mail.
Periods raised like Braille
on pages of poems turned over
done as pancakes on Sunday morning
& consumed while reading
about a new biography of Wallace Stevens,
something about its radiance –
or was it his? – and radiance also
in the second or third movement
of a concerto by Shostakovich
who has since gone to his grave
in all seriousness having rewritten
for the State
all his previous, frivolous
melodies. Some talk at Christmas!
(Some don't.) Some are free too early
with Merry Christmas, your reply lacking
a note of finality because you know you
will return many times: refuse closure
in any way, shape, or form. Meantime
things happen and people can suddenly
find themselves alone, powerless, & invisible.
They give their children pretty names
that become a sound among other sounds
when the service club Santa hands out
the Christmas present.
Coloured lights outline windows & doors,
turn the monkey tree into a carnival

of itself, pleased & demure under the crown of lights
installed in a pouring rain, heavy, mercury-laden
drops that hurt, slashing past the streetlights.

❋ ❋ ❋ ❋ ❋

What excitement awaits us
as we go for a Sunday drive
across the border, the yellow fields
of the river deltas full of cows
& fundamentalists. *God!* wanted everything
to be the way it is. *God!* wants you
to send your money now.
Small brown birds line the tree branches
like a Christmas carol, traffic flows
past the red exemplary barns
of the Fraser Valley.
God is a profusion of exactnesses
inside a phone with bad connections:
Hello? Hello? The words *Please* and *No*
coming through most clearly. Erma Bombeck's
a better read than the Bible, Freud, or
Marx as far as useful
& reassuring goes, and why shouldn't
art console? God is a text residing
between the lines & some are nervous
playing Name the Invisible. We exist as one
between pregnancies, otherwise inhabited
by a spirit whose limbs we watch
on the video screen as a play of darknesses
in the water. This is the head, this is a leg,
this pulsing smudge is the heart.
Or a string of smudges in the case of
a litter, Mother Cat with transmitters
on her belly. Sea rose, sea iris, sea lily:

three sisters of a mystical landscape
revealed by H.D., who named her child Perdita,
imagine. Girls were dragged
kicking & screaming out of the convents
to go back home after the Reformation.
The lucky ones eventually returned
to live out their days *virgo intacta*
but nobody new was allowed to enter.
This was in Nuremberg,
coming over the radio, dial glowing turquoise
an exclamation mark in the room's twilight
splicing the day's news, bites
of information whose spectacular triteness resembles
The Rape of the Lock. Good topics
between the lies and the management of lying:
break-ins, files stolen, ugly plans.
All information so far incomplete, merely
hearsay.

❀ ❀ ❀ ❀ ❀ ❀

Of nature and of man relax
the bond & language breakdances
the invisible, the yellow arrows
pointing towards town. In the
little hollow of Sleepy Dell
there once lived … and so on.
A story about exchange, pleasure,
and deprivation. All a dream
to us with quotation marks
around the real, plus possessions
and opinions and the hastened expunging
of desires suited
to an obsolete cosmology.
The municipal ego travels

in certain circles untroubled
by doubt, most problems lassoable
or hypnotized away by smiles,
but what about the murder victims
in the family homes and outside them
on the grass? To change
the subject, ornamental facades
are back with a vengeance, even though
our pictorial muscles are not
what they used to be.
Houses, one to a lot. Green
surrounds, car out front.
The changeling light does not change
the facts. One of those salads with green
jelly in a circle (celery, two apples,
carrots, a package of chopped walnuts)
for New Year's, the alleys patrolled by
dump trucks full of pebbles that
make a prodigious sound as they issue
into the wheelbarrows of Angelini's
Drainage. A new house going up,
piles of dead-looking dirt surround.
Someone's wash on the line straddles
a frozen garden, grotesque spikes
of Brussels sprouts, mad-hatter growths
of cabbage and broccoli, blackened
under a cold breath's beard of frost.
The stones clatter, wet ground gapes.

❀ ❀ ❀ ❀ ❀ ❀ ❀

New Year's passes.
The dishes are cleared away,
relatives waving goodbye through car windows.
The dog sick

from too much dark-meat turkey &
last night's storm departed
leaving a freshened landscape,
resolution joggers. The scene
of family, friends ripples out
to meet a smooth monopoly
of event, flat surface of a pond
in which ducks propel
by invisible motors
their high-riding tail feathers,
grunting as they go. Signs say
Do Not Feed them but they will
be fed. Beyond, the ocean glimmers
large & predictable, like Father,
with small boats in his pockets
placed there by children
who enjoy his giant body,
climb him like trees. He permits
the delusion that they are
stronger, and then the moment of truth
as they speed past their dreams
downward. The hour arrives,
the program changes, marked
by rolling credits. Couples kiss
in the toothpaste ad or throw a football
around. Everyone falls
to join the big heap, all breaths
confidently intertwined. Music
accompanies this infantile proposition
& others like it, even when the sound
is turned down they move
to a certain rhythm dictated by millions.
The stores are open & this is freedom.
Christmas toys break after
two hours of use but
any time of night or day

you can get another just the same.
In a cardboard box, then a plastic bag.
Machines cut the softwood,
the logger guiding the robot
by remote control to the tree it embraces
& cleanly murders, severing top and bottom
& laying it down in a heap with the others.
A large & unaccustomed
light gets larger as trees fall
& sky widens.

❀ ❀ ❀ ❀ ❀ ❀ ❀ ❀

Imagine a white CorningWare thermos
blocking the view of the traffic
on Macdonald Street, the dark roofs of houses
beyond. Mull over the small flood
in the basement, the American football games
on TV. Accept the dinner invitation
for jambalaya happily. The Saturday *Globe and Mail*
details the extinction of species in Sec. D,
Old MacDonald's farm a former rainforest
near the Amazon, scientific cattle
incipient cuts of hamburger beef, Lean
Cuisine while it rains all winter
in Prince George & my mother says
It makes me nervous. Dear Mom,
my little cactus collection
thrives on top of the file cabinet
but none of them bloomed at Christmas.
Ee-yi-ee-yi-oh. The night's dreams
persist into day, writer as satyr
in the front seat of a taxi aroused
& full of intent, remembered
dreams not black & white but the colour

of a rainy night, dreams *noirs*.
Or dreams *blancs*, blank for the right-hand
side of the page I write,
the hand I used to smoke with. Smoke
indicating misty realms in which we wave
our hands around, explaining something.
Smoke that coils under the hat brims
of lonely detectives. Secrets & unknowing,
that continues. Don't know much about
his-tory, don't know much
bi-*ol*-ogy. Going in & out of rooms,
making the bed, putting on the *Goldberg
Variations*, then the CBC.
The turquoise globe tilts towards the east.
My imaginary red beret matches my imaginary
red stockings, a walking signal
to the Resistance.
The underground is brightly lit,
is Hades of an entrepreneurial spirit
full of misery imports from horrible countries,
thin shiny garments hanging on mannequins
whose bony hips are slung
with silver belts, meagre Madonnas
remote and on tiptoe,
their white oval faces
stamped with hope, passivity, and sorrow.

❄❄❄❄❄❄❄❄

Myriad raindrops cling to myriad twigs
on the neighbour's birch tree, the neighbour
actually three, two sisters and a brother
each a blond, none of them
home very much. Their front-yard tree
like a large weed wending

its lanky crooked way upward
in the forest, a mere stick
you'd never notice. Still, it touches
the way trees in the city do, a place
in us that lives in books & dreams
that we forget & have to be reminded
to hug our kid. Go to cleaners.
Phone so & so. Pick up milk & bread,
toilet paper, dog food. Everything
impossible to put off even on Sunday
which seems to be a colder day
than any other and gives you time
for the personals: what we do
and say, and what settles between
like don't bother with those dishes,
I'll do them later. Or the sound
of your voice talking long-distance
to your mother that I hear
on my way inside from out, rain-soaked and
already hungry this time of day.
How was it? you say. The sky
uniform as a lid over the whole town,
everyone someone's neighbour.
Still, you give me the news from Ann Arbor
(Bob Arbor's sister,
comic-strip heroine, lady lawyer
of the '50s with soft hair & tweed suit,
lives with ailing mother
who weeps into the counterpane
on her bed by the window, a birch tree
outside, myriad raindrops clinging
to its bare thin branches
where late the sweet birds sang).
The daily is an engine of these
and other particulars, exactnesses
like the way you sit on the sofa

with that book that pen
and will never again
sit in that way, that light, just so
many grey hairs in your hair as today,
how many peels it took
to peel your morning orange.

❀ ❀ ❀ ❀ ❀ ❀ ❀ ❀ ❀ ❀

Eagerness to go but reluctance
because of the weather
creates a small contretemps inside me.
It occupies for a while
a need for indecision,
starts a fresh surveillance
of external signs that used to be called
superstition. Don't ask me
what propels things from A to B,
why some people were in the hotel at 3 p.m.
when the fire started & others
were down at the beach. The vain,
the scrupulous – getting out of the sun,
writing postcards home
before the last mail truck leaves.
Fires in the tropics no longer seem redundant,
it's no cooler than elsewhere, flames
diluted by the heat of sun. And the tinderbox
of outrage and indebtedness sitting
to the south, and south of that
whole hemispheres of outrage
led by mothers who're told
they must rely on the Pope to reinforce
a thing or two once or twice
a decade, otherwise they're on their own.
How different they are from us

I say, speaking of the French in movies,
how I envy their emotional freedom
& their clothes, their kisses
the size of documentaries.
The way they talk on their nice phones
you can tell they are undiminished
by technology. The Divine Fools
who live on our corner
& drive rainbow-coloured vehicles
will soon see me pass
with a black umbrella
over my head & a letter in my hand,
stamp shining in the upper-right corner,
as the day dims and vapours accumulate
on McKenzie Heights.
The last of the Christmas trees
have been undressed and discarded
in the alleys.
I spoke to ours, I said Thanks,
you smelled great, your beauty
made us happy. Imagine bringing a tree
in the house to adorn with coloured lights
and tiny birds and bending angels –
to offer our anxious gifts to, sacrifices
of love and obligation.

SIX

1. AHHHH ...

Sunday painters, these
gardeners

who bend
at the waist

to water and soil
and seedlings
by the dozen

poke infant plants
into the ground
pat around & presto

green

2. AXE MURDERER

Look out!
Run!

Here he comes
dragging his axe.

He drags it because
he is so evil & stupid
he cannot hold it up

Unlike the whistling woodcutter
who lives in the little log house.

Chop chop, chop chop
goes the axe.

Eek! and O my God!
say the trees and the women.

But all this goes on
in the forest.

So you can relax.

3. RESPONSIVE

You can do it the easy way
or you can do it the hard way.

The hard way, the hard way.

4. CONTRETEMPS

On the way
he said
what he said

During
he did
what he did

Coming back
we spoke
not a word

After
I sold
what I could

5. ROSARY

In small rivers
of hours
passing

words grab
as fingers
spread the air

when leaning
down to stretch
interior ligaments

that pull at, hurt
a little
behind the mind –

It feels good
to do this & breathe
coming up

counting pebble
by pebble
my spine

6. SUMMER

The house is built
day by day
quickly, the trucks

come & go
with shirtless operators
cranes & gears

the roof on
(prefab)
in one morning

now the pale yellow
siding, imitation brick
along the front

it is obviously
grand, he is
proud, entering

the unfinished
front door, a small
uncomplaining man

to look over
his day's work,
try the lights.

BEING ADULTS

1. MAKING A BREAK

An open space signals
where the cat
does his business
in a far corner
of the yard, facing
the mountains,
the doctor's BMW
etherized in the alley.

Thinking of this broken-up sky
where the long wind slams around
raising to a pitch & billows
our lovely wants, as
desire is too serious –

like the cement truck
that shifts gears in vain
when the light goes green.

2. SAVED

Last night my young friend and I
talked about bullfights while I
sought in vain for a word
that comes to me now: *Minotaur*.
My young friend is newly aware
of the Devil – St. Paul
he says with his lovely mouth,
in Ephesians, he says
with his shoulders & everything
across from me – & I am angry
with my friend.

3. ADULTS

Being adults
we share our toys.
Nothing is better
than this. This
delicate sliding out
of the pickup stick
from the small chaos
on the floor. On our knees
feet going to sleep
we bend towards
an intense operation.
Outside this intimacy
construction companies
lurch & sigh in muddy trucks
around the work site.
Human voices shout
over the sound of internal
combustion engines.
Things are dug up,
things are dumped out.
Diagrams
of what works, all the arrows
pointing in the same direction,
their immaculate detours
notwithstanding.

4. NEW YEAR'S

Apparently sane
with my New Year's Eve
hairdo, as the cab

is coming around
eight. No exit –

but these threads
are black & gold,
shine hard
when lights
are low, so

see you on the
windswept heath
my heart, she
chatters,
will hold up
her proper end
of things, e.g.

the conversation,
her sweet chain-mail
evening bag, his imaginary
French kiss.

Interspersal 3

THE WATERMELON

The clock said 10 to 3.

I went upstairs, wrote lines, crossed them out.

I felt the weight of one of those gas masks on my spirit.

My spirit. My size 7 ½ shoe.
My Canada Life insurance policy.

Everywhere I look,
books.

I suppose Sharon Olds has just finished another
fabulous poem about her child's tender scalp.

Poetry: I couldn't care less.

Long lines, short lines:
two ways of suffocation.

The current stops,
thought loops back on itself.

Last night's dream drifts around
like coloured smoke.

I've always loved rivers. Music.

Thoughts, sayings, about what goes on.
What I hear and think I know.

Poetry makes me feel like drinking too much.
I wish I was a man.

If I was someone else, would I prefer
their troubles to my own?

I would still wash my face & comb my hair,
reach for briefcase
open at the top with some xeroxing sticking out,
put on my coat, go out to the car.

There's nothing tropical about me.

The Occasions

————

Gala Roses

————

From Toledo

THE OCCASIONS

> Men have talked about the world
> without paying attention to the world
> or to their own minds, as if
> they were asleep or absent-minded.
> —Heraclitus, tr. Guy Davenport

Are dim. Are a missing
of the mark. Are pretty
Chinese lanterns, fireworks
I woke to thinking
someone was stealing the piano.
Are the piano itself:
Moments musicaux
fall out of the window, scatter
like memory all over everything.

In the Public Garden someone bends
over the roses. But for the polar bears,
orangutans, sea otters,
purple-ass baboons, the giraffe,
crocodiles, peacocks, the killer whale,
the zoo is deserted. Under the water
creatures blink and eat.

These pale pink roses
are the tenderest things.
The palest alabaster pink.
Sitting with them you understand
the perfection of all things.

Moments later amnesia, rubato
of a phrase of light.

2.

The phone rings, hauling you up
out of a dream. You are light-headed,
unreal, addicted to whatever
keeps you going. Books, coffee,
poetry, someone's voice.

Across town the carpenters
lay down their tools &
drive away in dusty Thunderbirds
to a meeting in the stadium.
Someone explains his situation
at the Food Bank. Someone else
closes the curtains & opens the Scotch.
The intermittent sun
exhales a yellow breath.
Clockwise, tiny black aphids
race around the convolutions
of a rose someone aims at
with a spray gun.

The convolutions of the rose
suggest an ecstasy
untroubled by too much meaning.

Or too little.

Outside the Hudson's Bay
the Hare Krishnas are hopping
and chanting: unburdened,
ecstatic, their blue invisible deities
laugh in the air.

3.

Greek Day. The Pericles Society
souvlaki stand runs out early.
Solemn bouzouki bands
repeat themselves in faster measures
for the young men who dance,
naked insteps flashing among the swords,
handsome conceited heads flicking
to the left and the right.
Old mothers in black click & talk
the meat smoke rises
as if from ancient battlegrounds.
Heraclitus, dog-bitten old ghost
admonishes the crowd
to wake up & share a world
as a small plane
trailing a river of plastic words
progresses round the sky.

4.

Speaking English
we go over & over
the things that happen,
but I would rather have you
in my arms than in this conversation.

Desire and ineptitude
commit themselves to memory –
it's hard not to regret
anything. For example,
coldness, a pretended indifference.
The heart transformed
to a battery.

Pairs of women
lean over restaurant tables
talking. They know everything.
Their perfume recalls to them
a certain gesture in the back seat
of a taxi in Toronto that said
I agree to this.

They fiddle with their earrings,
sufficient unto themselves
in pale summer dresses
like women who wait
for a war to end.

Or the shrimp boats
to come in. So why don't you
hurry home. The windows
are open: one to the east
& one to the west. Sirens
in the cross-breeze,
novels on the bed.

GALA ROSES

after reading Michele Leggott

If it's not flowing I'll not tell

not to ask me either under the lilac nor upon the bedspread

a secret fig green orb a mouth the size fills

inside perfectly & juice a slight muscular taking

a trout in the boat under the sun's

tremor the sly slight feather the fisherman strokes

words upon you oh body oh stone lintel and maiden frieze

lifting high the garland gala roses white lilies

legs draped heavy satin sitting heads crowned braided

sung & caught by nets your sheer wings beauty

her gateway fig-mouth and trout so slips down

Was fast the shift to blankness the nape of neck's

adorable space many catastrophes could & have befallen

axes have fallen upon fair bent heads still speaking

don't think about it don't listen the dog is advised re

the nature of his operation & moans of pity no no

refuse to be bitter neither will he nor she all

friends & happy in the skin of some accommodation stretched

beyond bearing goes loose in the mind – covered saint-like

in arrows walking to work not screaming not yelling a kind word

the mailman the butcher the old woman rambling alone book in hand

kerchief & housedress a pocketful of amethysts & quartz crystal

Orange silk triangles shine from the Berber kilim

green & blue oasis water sweetness pregnant moon adrift

large above the stucco the pointed rooflines grave

& magnificent occasions *it feels so good* entwined you my

darling my sweetheart the years each one lost to us

added on to sorrow's sad amazed boat nudging nudging

the wharf's oily edge blackened posts wavering

moon-blackened water's profound & frightful mirror

led here by what sure-footedness *quietness & passion*

with or without him it them you see you big whatevers

going in and out like breathing I can't help it

Form follows whitely next the big tree shaded

fruitless not full of speeches like King Lear apoplectic

upholstered beneath the tent of his rent sub-

conscious we read as libretto to folly and lust

virtue's adventure high above nodding

here there to them below dirty-faced with cockney spraddle

good sense good rhymes or not-bad chocolate bar

some poor guy had to leave during the storm scene

passing knees in near tears mine also that people

idiotic in castles' granite chill behind the unicorns

draperies & trumpets strumpets waggle hips

blue skirts the young princes point at

Sour cream egg whites coconut icing sugar mountainous

sweetness missing the book of favourites my lord and saviour

wants me for a sunbeam others too but I sing me he wants me

eye beams coiled on the violets riverbank pregnant

by mandrake root or thought *two hearts two hearts that beat*

as one covered over the site with leaf mould undid the night

pointed the way down the aisle's little footpath lites

two fingers each hand point to the exits

jumping into heaven's thought clouds blue peace cold wind

floating throne river of stars the big lap

and book the white chest, odour of father comes now

Illumination marches thoughtless around in shorts

watch out where you're going map turned this way

that way north switched to south

and back to north again knocked

off-course *within human memory* Velikovsky imagines Venus

came so close she threw the earth off its spinning hence

concussive reeling waters slop beehives coil whales dive

ant colony exudes itself a greyish pile by the roadside's

hairpin turn lake blasting blue & huge mountainous cold

planet of *seas and vapours, mud, fire, and dust*

Red head of rose partitions the vase lip

he gave me relaxed on the porch charming bare

arm offering sweet muscles long cursive I'll take

too then taking took mine so entwined twinned arms oh

well the picnic today so fry chicken all morning

dip egg dip crumbs lay down in the brilliant cooking

ocean floating things persons dog-paddling

old & sandy muzzled sneezing wagging creature full

moon moaning through clouds & trees she chants

the puzzle of the blessed virgin's virginity but

things do happen Emma Laraine's daughter smiling due November

Tristes tropiques bristle of boat stems at the yacht club

ocean sways round turquoise peaks long as Indonesia

tips obscured toes dipped in the sea for a feeling of *out*

there we made it to maybe we'll go somewhere we'll

be okay as of this day at the park looking

for a familiar posture or hair or gesture on the green

nice to see so many families jungle gyms hibachi smoke

weather-talk clouds clearing the breaking in two

and into twos the coil of something – helpless resemblance

& architecture of long-forgotten desire remaining an *in-depth*

report HELP ME bottle bobbing its message too late probably

Tone is something to take in the lake whose arms

embrace peninsulas of trees teepees canoes and strings

of hung smoked fishes all in the museum The Museum

of Love and of What Is Pretty, purchases from abroad *foreign*

merchandise said the American grandma from her wing chair 93

pushes the plate-glass door to the early-bird sitting

open herself expecting to find things

not to her liking: the tune on the player piano.

On her dictionary flyleaf in blue ink *nostalgia*

arthritis recluse royal expanse of lawn out the window

should have been peacocks too but their cries hurt she

never stopped loving her third husband the one

who looked like Spencer Tracy

Green machine beyond the ruby dahlias & empty

town without you-him-it a gap thinking fills overflows

scrolled as music coiling out the mouth of the alto

love's refrain ornamented Elizabethan *garden*

wall where stars are bright imagination hides her purple

violets *such sweet sorrow* striates the mind like bar codes

dragged over a dark star a price appearing or someone

at the door with a seven-rap tattoo shave-and-a-haircut

the drag queens' audience drab by the default's wild

fuchsia gloves silver gowns mountainous Bo-Peep wigs

the gallantry stiff shoulders and exaggerated mouth of her

continuous birth.

FROM TOLEDO

From the twelfth to the fifteenth centuries, versions of *El Cant de la Sibil·la* (*The Song of the Sibyl*) were performed in cathedrals throughout the Iberian peninsula at Christmas matins, most often by a boy dressed in a tunic, oversleeves, and gloves, and sometimes wearing a wig and "a hairy tail which gave him the appearance of a mermaid." The Sibyl was often the last in a "procession of the prophets" bearing witness to the Day of Judgment.

An autumn
flower arrangement
arrives, light rain
pestering the garden
falling into brown decay
until spring, that
far-off moment. The song
of the sibyl blew into the cavernous
cathedral as I opened the door
to a woman delivering flowers.

I had just unrolled a mauve
shag rug downstairs.
Loops of wool I could
slip a finger through, wed
myself to a carpet groom.
And me a cloth person clad
in sweaters and fleece, feet
submerged in fluff.

The sibyl laments the
Day of Judgment, the splitting
& rending of the Earth like a piece
of old blue cloth in the hands
of wrath, puffs of dust rising
from the rip lines.

From Toledo, the Spanish town
in whose cathedral the sibyl sang,
I have a pair of golden scissors inlaid
with a scrolling pattern. The cathedral –
one of many we saw that year, that
decade – the decade of the pewter goblet
received for years of service at work –
and stored in a cupboard in its lizardy
protective case.

The sybil's song takes me to poetry,
that coughing sister, the one in bed
using up her sick days. A soft old cloth
folded and warmed in the oven
is pressed to her Vicks-slick chest,
a benediction. ·

Imperial trumpets announce another verse.
We steel ourselves for more bad news.

The pewter goblet for years of service at the blackboard
diagrams the soul's journey, so to speak,
with spirals and connotations. I defend
the meaning of texts and would like to say that
all interpretations are a matter
of possibilities endlessly recycled
within the one Possibility.

The flower arrangement is set on the table.
Dark reds, deep yellows. Another refrain
cites the end of the world, the terrors of Judgment
Day, the splitting & rending,
the wishing one were dead – and finishes with the sound
of a bell and more trumpets
touting their own representation
of pagan intrusions, pagan self-esteem.

We can't be too
walking-on-eggshells when it comes
to the Sibyl: a boy in sleeves and gloves.

S/he emerges, sings, leaves
the scene or is absorbed in the many
voices of the people.

Her/his mantilla, cloak, jewels,
gown, the cloth at the waist are
a folded dimension aslant her sightlines.

Many *amens* signal her departure
from this Christmas night & the arrival of the next
prophet. We've been waiting
a long time. Now the newer music,
the variations, the furrowed interpretations.
Now the standing up once more, the trouble
of coats and boots, someone coughing, the tired
choir, the awaited moment –
its shine.

Interspersal 4

CLEMATIS MONTANA RUBENS

While asleep I dreamed the world had changed.

All there was to eat was some kind of dismal soup.
To be free we had to hide in a skyscraper.
Police shone flashlights at us in the car,
like nazis spending a long time on each face.

City hall was corrupt, gangsters laughed
at the mayor.

Nighttime or twilight, plus rain, was all there was.

Fortunately it was just a dream
and by 9:30 sleepy teams had gathered at the park for playoffs

and in a lone spot a martial artist: one arm then another
towards a bush, like pistons.

On the car radio someone says *montana rubens* is her favourite
clematis – pale-pink blossoms in April and May

masses of pale fragrant blossoms.

At a red light I turn towards the back seat
and tell the dog he is a good boy.

SHARON THESEN READS "CLEMATIS MONTANA RUBENS"

youtu.be/fv8ynZsmAMg

Parts of Speech

———

I Drive the Car

PARTS OF SPEECH

1. THE

The crossings
out the
cancelling
of rages
too violent to be
borne the
dullness that
ensues the
world a rubber
object between
the teeth the difficult
recovery from
being loved
hard as it was, then
& now
the feeling circuits
disconnected
at the source
& language itself the jape
when separate
is one word

2. TO SEE

How long
is not seeing
possible
or

too much
to say

we "want" each other

then what
is the problem

between the gaze
& the window
your eyes & mine

3. THIS & THAT

Look at that mountain. That must be Shasta Mountain.
Look at those clouds over there, I'll bet it's raining
down there. That woman shouldn't be sitting in the smoking
section if she needs oxygen. I'm going to ask the stewardess
if she can be moved up to the non-smoking section. I don't
really like Canadian Club, I'm more used to Seagram's.
Let me know when the stewardess comes down here, I'm going
to say something to her. I suppose nobody can smoke now for
the whole trip. If someone is that sick they should be
in the non-smoking section in the first place. Excuse me,
can the woman with the oxygen be moved up to the non-smoking
section? It's not really fair to us here you know. No? Well,
okay, I guess we'll just have to suffer. Hey look, she's
getting her lunch before anyone else but how's she supposed
to eat with the mask on her face, oh, they're taking it off.
I guess she must be feeling better. Boy, it takes all kinds.
I feel sorry for her though. Would you mind holding my glass?
I got to go. Doesn't look like there's a lineup too bad yet
but just wait till after lunch!

4. USAGE

Do not read these words.
There are too many words written
already. It's all been said
before, everyone knows that.
There are 31 stories, or 29, or 42.
Everything is the same old story.
All you have to do is
pick up your daily newspaper
& there they are,
the same old stories.
Words everywhere. A trillion
trillion words laid end to end
would stretch around the globe
a hundred times. Equators
of words, ropes
tying the world up tight,
creasing the oceans & strangling you
in your bed at night.
Dear reader, take heed &
by the way,
will you marry me?

5. PERSON PLACE OR THING

Out the window
here & there a
flash of sprinklers,
three birds
on the wire
sing. The view being
from the second storey

to the left the birds
the sprinklers
to the right a length
of quiet room, a bed
& books laid out
against the wall.

Like those twisting strands
of water, hair
across a sleeping face
that drowns in a dream.

The empty lawn chair floats
in a sea of green & dandelions
the sky above you you
do not see.

6. THE ARGUMENT BEGINS WITH A

Love,
whoever do you
resemble.
Not a snake,
not a thing
in the dark.
Your appearance
brings dread to the heart,
knowledge
unasked for.
In the lamplight
your eyes are green
your inevitable wound
is red. A brown moth
pins herself
against the wall,
her wings are hers
unwished for.
Wing & heart
slide towards each other
along a trajectory
called love, exchange
for a moment,
their properties. A wing-shaped
heart. A heart-shaped
wing. A breathing stillness. A
motionless weight.

7. AFTER SPICER

The imaginative
composition by the
imaginative writer.
Puts words to a sword
in the heart,
makes a picture.
A feeling. Real blood
on real spoons
we take out of our mouths.
The soup,
of heroes. The blood
in Byron's mouth,
my mother's mouth.
The silver spoon
we aren't born with
& the silver tongue
we die with
between sentences
between lovers

8. MAGIC

Appearances are everything.

If you ask me no questions
I'll tell you no lies.

Dyslexia
lurks around the corner,
can make you write backwards
or not at all.

The mind
runs its tongue
around itself, tries
a phrase or two.
Wonders
if it came from the dyslexic
in the blue suit or
the younger one
in the red T-shirt
who has just appeared.

Famous dyslexics
include detectives
& brilliant stars
like Betelgeuse and Rodney Kidd.

You may be a carrier &
not know it.
You may never write backwards
or not at all
& not know it

when whammo! it
suddenly appears, & it's
on instead of no
tra instead of art
ouy instead of you
em instead of me

ouy em on tra
& all that light.

9. ECHOLOCATION

My son asks me
which do you think
is the smartest,
whales or humans?

& I answer,
humans.

Chittering,
chittering. Noisy & hopeless
monuments to some
endless TV show

& though we can't see the moon
for the crap in the sky, we get TV pictures
of the moons of Saturn
previously unheard of

         & *The Gong Show*
via Anik II &
Stayfree Mini Pads, the absurdity
absorbed, this is consciousness
now

    shooting across Pacific skies
over the cold & heaving waves
the whales move through, deep
under the shadow of a boat full of scientists
reaching out with diverse instruments
to capture the chittering
sublunar subaquatic
talk.

I DRIVE THE CAR

I drive the car
while the choir ascends
to a far transparency
these words tap at
with a show of politeness

I drive my car
and my friend also drives hers
& takes a detour to watch crows assemble
& disperse over the Cassiar Connector

They live there

I drive the car
afraid of the earthquake
& drive it
afraid of myself, what is it I
do, I wonder, & also what
others do, are they also
afraid?

Or else go crazy I drive the car
around in that
too like a maniac, like the wind

In the car someone's playing the piano
with an eye patch on & the helium
voice of a stoned poet, Bésame mucho,
& *muchos federales*
at the border

Where you can't step out
past a certain line painted
across the pavement and why would you
anyway, enter that foreign country
all aplomb & curiosity

No, I drive the car.
I hope it works, that the engine
doesn't fall apart. I think
oh, it will last five or ten years.
Then what. Another car.

My car I drive back & forth
around the town over bridges & here
and there, like everyone else
driving their cars. In the back seat
sits the ghost of your grandma.

I drive the car & pick up my friend
at her house, she comes out
the red door, I'm five minutes late
& we're laughing tragically by the time we
go past the SPCA.

The road is black after dark rain
and it ends in the sea. Big semis
are Minotaurs, some have smokestacks.
The air stings from tiny black particles
they blow their horns at, burdened and in a hurry

I put her in drive
& then I drive her & this
is what I do, I drive
the car.

Interspersal 5

THE PARROT

She flew, she was up
& gone, they had let her out
for a treat & were sorry now.
Red tail feathers
way, way up in a fir tree
on the side of a mountain.
It was north. Crows
eyed her. Way, way down
the people were making
little pyramids of peanuts &
calling her name: Isabel! Isabel!
They clicked tongues
and whistled, went away and
came back later. The sun got large
and red, turned the heat up
under her vocabulary. Hey Sailor!
Good Golly Miss Molly! Want
A Cracker? So What!
The crows backed off
& stared, diamond bracelets dangling
from their beaks. All that night
the parrot prayed & sang,
in the morning it was over.
She glided downward, branch
to spiky branch. The people
wept and applauded, rushed her
back to her cage exhausted,
the undisputed champion
of the air. She was never the same
after that. The vet said it was

a bit like the cave scene
in *A Passage to India* – something
to do with language, the dark, &
existence. Stupendous!
the parrot kept saying for years
after & the crows invented a dream.

Confabulations

CONFABULATIONS

I still believe that bad French wine was my nemesis.
I began to improve slightly when I took to rum and
gave up taking vitamins.

> —Malcolm Lowry
> February 1949, Dollarton, BC

When the fire devours itself, when the power turns
against itself, it seems as if the whole being is made
complete at the instant of its final ruin and that the
intensity of the destruction is the supreme proof, the
clearest proof, of its existence.

> —Gaston Bachelard
> *The Psychoanalysis of Fire*
> Translated by Alan C.M. Ross

Malcolm Lowry
Late of the Bowery
His prose was flowery
And often glowery
He lived, nightly, and drank, daily,
And died playing the ukulele.

—Malcolm Lowry
Selected Poems of Malcolm Lowry (1962)

A dove-grey morning
soon to turn blue
as lights go out
& silent movie begins
broken projector
flapping celluloid
mind's guts churning
sweating nervous erratic
guilt, it's okay
nothing wrong I could forget
it if I could remember it
legs & arms loosened out
mouth talking
fall back fast dissolve
a light snow falling in the room.

At the bottom of the garden
the hidden bottle. He makes
a rectitudinous beeline
for it, plain as day
his casualness an effort.
The heat spreading
everywhere, his mind
up to tricks his face
won't believe.
His stiff walk,
bones poisoned.
How he loves it all,
the amorous snake
in the amorous grass,
the disgusted neighbour
watering fruit trees
is his best friend.
The distant tequila the key
to the day, the beauty
of all things burning
through whitened glass,
his open heart
a surgical instrument.

Bacchus is not
the god in this case,
innocent & vulgar –
nor demon. Spirit
a magical language
binds community
sunders same.
Spirit resembling love
hence saboteur
of same. Sweet shortcut
to quote unquote hell
through a private
blinded paradise, *spiritus
contra spiritum.*

His ex-heart
speaking to the woman
they call the Blessed
Virgin is busy
making deals.
He's caught up in,
in love with
the exaltation
of the error
of his ways
outside the circle
outside the unmoved
& unmoving given.
He prays anyway
for love of life
at least, among
the flickering candles
beneath the serene
blue folds of her gown
his thick tongue
beating the words
behind his teeth:
I have sunk low.
Let me sink lower still.

White walls sweat flies
move fast as trains.

Gripping the counter's edge
to wait it out.

Watch the little maelstrom
in the draining sink,
the mindless unfaltering
laws-of-nature
vortex. *His steps
teetered to the left,
he could not make them
incline to the right.*

It was the dark.

The dark cantina
adjacent to the Bus Terminal
where lived
the widow Gregorio
and his debt
of five centavos.

Stooping over the half-hidden
Tequila Añejo de Jalisco
& waving to the neighbour
he mentions the weather
& also
he's on the wagon.
The funeral wagon
I'd say, glares Mr. Quincey.
In any case
more sober when drunk
than sober.
There are three
standing on the balcony,
even the raggy sunflower
is erect & opprobrious.
He resents their
incessant nervous
watchfulness.
He's afraid
they think he's a liar.

The five attractive garter snakes
assemble for the concert.
He's found their tastes
run to the gloomy.
His ukulele twanging out
hymn tunes
in diminished sevenths.
The pink grass swaying.
The clouds farting thunder.
The butterfly caught
in the jaws of the cat,
pulsing wings
frantic emerald curtains.

Should I say
Malcolm, your name
is the sound
of clam tracks,
the knock of kelp
on rock? Or Clarence,
wooden matches hissing
at nightfall?

There you would be
sitting on the clam-hole beach
in the noonday sun
& two seconds later
your house is in flames.
Again. Gin and manuscripts
snatched from the hellfire
always at your heels
panting & fanged.

Correspondences
too creepy to ignore.
Or maybe just bad
ventilation, rotten
luck. You were right
about a lot of things –
this world
scissored your mind,
bone-dry shreds of ecstasy
& terror igniting
your fragile nests.

Mea culpa.
And the culprit
is my mother,
the nanny
who tried to smother me
one day on the cliff,
the Syphilis Museum
on Paradise Road,
my diseased eyes,
Bellevue where they put me,
my immense
imagination.
The only books in the house
Inebriety by Crabbe,
Conrad Aiken's *Blue Voyage*
(maybe two or three others).
Mea culpa.
The doctor says
manic-depressive, says
compulsive neurosis
the alcohol a mask.
Language the mask –
pelado – peeled –
now it takes me
up to a whole afternoon
to find the word
I need.

On the third boozeless day he rose,
virtue restored. Publishers
written to. A long, less
wibberley wobberley walk
along the beach rocks.
The delicate white haze
outside now, flattened zinc
coin of sea & sun a platinum
wavering disc.
Wharf creaking in the wake
of a tug, ferns
soaking up stones. The world
his oyster.
"Welcome home," my wife
smiles, greeting me.
"Ah yes, my darling, it really is
home now. I love those curtains
you made."

So why not a visit to our old friend
the bootlegger
on so fine an afternoon?

The dripping path grows
pitch black. Some dogs howl
at an absent moon, no drunk
tells time. A flashlight
beam from the dead
of night finds him sprawled
on the forest floor
gobbling ferns –

spitting spores
around the names
of constellations
crawling the sky.

He stands his back
to her, bare torso
outlined by sea & fir trees.
The callused tops of his hands
behind him kneading
& rubbing at the table top
he leans against,
three packs a day voice
addressing the abyss
his wife writing it down.

The shakes so bad can't hold
a pen or pencil anymore
won't eat
needs help getting dressed

The writing body
flashing one-sided headache,
eczema on lower limbs,
heartbeat erratic,
weight loss,
blank dreams,
fatigue an invisible thief
peels away the days
at night alternating coma
& transmitter.

Ferris wheel revolves
backward into black night
with Lowry the lone rider
vomiting mescal sideways
across the contrary circle
of fiesta-coloured lightbulbs

Where I am it is dark.

I fear the worst & alas my only friend
is the Virgin for those who have nobody with
& she is not much help.

I am being spied upon by five policemen
in black sunglasses. All day long
a vulture stares at me
from around the wash basin.
While I purify my sorrow.

Márquez shot to death
in a stupid drunken argument –
or not – they took Márquez
out of his house one afternoon
and shot him, saying *you no wrider*
you an espider.
At the time he was shaving
fresh from siesta his white shirt
on the back of a chair
rungs showing through like bones
& suddenly the dog barking –

They arrest me for drawing maps on the bar
with a finger dipped in tequila –
communist, agitator, spy – plus
no passport.

Ugly voices spatter the street
with vowels of *la mordida.*

In Mexican prisons the third degree
is castration. They tried that
one fine night, unsuccessfully
I regret to say.

Later we ended up in the *zócalo*
guards & all, roaring with mescal
& everyone with blue faces.

They are looking for me yet.
I practise knots
on the fringe of her yellow shawl
its softness on my legs
striped with bars of shuttered light.

That last night in the cantina
with Yvonne & Hugh, spectral chicken
on the Day-of-the-Dead menu
the glasses of mescal appear &
disappear as if drunk by a ghost
– or did he? or was he – ever
in love with her –
his intolerable dear friends
their intolerable dear conversation
among the thunder
& from some puzzling distance –
the pimp eyeing him in the toilet stall
chewing a marzipan coffin offers him
a stone – here,
clean yourself with this –
talk of love, talk of war
& a dark symbolic horse rears up
against the storm.

El Farolito is deserted
except for a one-legged rooster
& a sleeping dog. The street
empties like a drain
into the *barranco*
where they threw the Consul's body.
Where they also throw
dead dogs & those they do not name
compañero, but rather,
pelado. Thief.

Bix Beiderbecke at noon.
Alternating soneryl and straight gin,
five, ten, twenty
versions of a sentence
annealed to one broken one.
Could be anywhere – the same sea
surrounds. Triumphant lucidity
of mind, the hand steady.
Everything behind him now.
The Voyage That Never Ends
swells by a page or two,
drifts north-northwest.

Restless. Soneryl.
Vitamin B. The heebie-jeebies.
Sleep for three hours dreaming
animals. *Dear Albert,*
there's at least two thousand pages more
of stuff. Forgive me.
I am murdered by the pistils
of mauve orchids in a white vase
while Bolshevik choirs sing
religious. Strychnine. Allonal.
A cumulonimbus cloud of
empty bottles builds in the sky,
the bruises French wine
the shiny spots mescal.
Forgive the tone of injured innocence,
but. Chloral. Straight rum.
Nosebleed like an opened tap
pouring into my hands, tossed
like roses at the cheering crowd.
Sodium Pentothal – I wake up
weeping the whole grief of the world
strangling my vocabulary.

Loathing Margerie
I would be dead
without her. I guess
I'd better let them
put me in the hospital
for a rest. Every day
she comes to see me
wearing high heels &
reading me censored letters.
Stayed put until I couldn't
stand it, went out one night,
a few days later
I'm in a white bed
dictating memories
to the doctor. Some of them
are pretty good
even if untrue.
I need to be told
there's a reason for this,
some word that will describe me
& set me free.

For a few days
I considered having the lobotomy
but Margerie & I
figured it was a bit extreme
& I'd never write again,
no never again.
I'd be in the past tense.

To be rescued from hell
you have to be in hell
so they put me
in some laboratory of it
& sit outside taking notes
every time I scream
nightmare & vomit.
Unlimited supply of gin
interrupted by injections
of apomorphine, a red lightbulb
burning constantly *to increase
the horror effect* he tells us
over his clipboard.
I was locked in.
Got so thirsty I drank my own piss,
went so crazy there are no words
for it except I saw angels
on fire, so vile
they were laughing at me.
It wasn't so bad.
Outlasted the guy before me
by five days the first time,
sixteen the next. Told them –
the stupid bastards –
I'd had the best time of my life.

The poets' lake country
the final cure,
sheep in pastures grazing
& Wordsworth's daffodils
exactly the host
he said they were – oh bleak
bleak days of separation
from self & catastrophic
states of mind.
He writes with a brave face
to the old fisherman in Dollarton
birthday wishes & fondest love.
They have found a lovely cottage
in the quiet village of Ripe
& listen to music on the radio
& walk and talk with the neighbours
sometimes,
go to The Lamb for a pint
or two or twenty –
Alone in the garden
after a violent night
he kisses the bright pink faces
of peonies along the fence
tasting bees & the hereafter.

You say you a wrider
but we read all your wridings
dey don't make sense
you no wrider
you an espider

where I am it is dark

A lot of rain falling
& wasted days
but a few gins
& I can still get off
a decent letter.
My personality comes & goes
like the mailman, however
& I can honestly admit
(at my age, how embarrassing)
that I have no idea
who I am. Was always
good at sea, though.
Without a storm
I'm useless.
Other than those
literary parties in New York
where they loved me,
they loved me not,
there's one thing
keeps coming back:
we're on our way
to the ferry terminal,
black hangover & arguing
inlet to the left
the morning stars & Margerie
suddenly quiet
puts her hands over her face
and starts to laugh, it somehow
all seems so comical.

Sideways conspiracy
detonates

all things for the mouth
shattered
sucking mother night
claimed
earth & stars, sea & fire

still
a mockingbird pipes
the morning in

Interspersal 6

SKYLARKS

Through the blue
recycling bags you can see the news
of yesterday, the smeared faces,
juice boxes, sheets of instructions.
Omens of a map of increasing
wateriness: the soul, according
to Heraclitus, should not
be moist, but rather,
dry. Down in the valley
sirens make a racket.
Now what? Some calamity & calamity
is really spelled *c-l-i-m-a-t-e*.
The thing the guys who know
are really sweating about. The thing
everybody knows unto the very ants
and skylarks.

The Fire

The Good Bacteria

THE FIRE

Mars glared
in the firmament
among the shooting stars
the orange moons

mornings cloaked
in terracotta
smoke, yellow pears
pendant in orchards

a fallen, roasted
aspen leaf
Etruscan artifact

among the tongs
and tines of suppertimes

Airplanes lumber
upward, unfold white silk sheets
of lake upon the woods

while the Armed Forces
unpack gear and smooth cots
in tidy tents in city parks

Gloom the breathing element
deposits a half-consumed *Time*
magazine on a parked car
at the mall

and scorched pages
from a first-aid manual: a victim
choking, a victim grasping

at straws, the weather
forecast, the percentage
chance of rain – this means

houses must be burning!

though the fire makes its
own weather anyway

ferocious wind storms

(her hair she demonstrated later
flew straight out in one direction
then suddenly equally straight out in the other direction
as she stood in the yard

and a walloping sound, otherwise
eerie quiet)

they left on bicycles fearing traffic panic

but everyone did go orderly
if terrified and if two followed
fanatic the other's tail lights all the way
to Starbucks speaking white-faced
into cellphones in the parking lot

I want the house clean
for the fire: to the greater
scourging I offer the lesser.

Windex, floor mop,
sink stopper polished with Vim,
the whole nine yards,
the whole ball of wax.

Last week we'd twirled Mars
to clarity inside
binoculars, discussed
its proximity, its palpable
redness. The likelihood
of "life," what, some weird-
looking worm or germ.

And this morning
the vacuum cleaner is travelling
along behind. I apologize

to a cushion, I can't take you
dear, like throwing a maiden
off a cliff, well, not quite

but the sense of propitiation
was there: Fire, here is a clean floor.
Fire, here is an innocent cushion.

A half-moon wears out the night sky,
buttonhole of a jean jacket
worried to thinness
while Mars
lounges among his rights

his stogie – a burning pine forest –
held out at arm's length in order to hear better
the appeals of the widows

            ↓

My arms feel unattached and threading
even the largest needle
I tremble and miss the eye.

The fallen-off button on a folded towel
near the iron in the quietness
of another house itself
now hazed with smoke

In the haste to pack, the button
had twirled and flipped, darkness
was about to fall

I bought flashlights
and a round case of needles
as if it were an ordinary errand

helicopters above the roof
sound like something being ground

on my lap the legs and arms
of the garment needing a button

↓

The thread moves to the right
or to the left like a barker's booth
at the circus where you throw softballs
at the passing ducks, it looks so easy

and you really want to win the large pink jaguar

Go ahead fire.
Dot with embers the patios
of citizens trying to dine al fresco

aim flamethrowers
at the forest service, the army,
the navy for that matter, who also came
to help

the exhausted and the holdouts, make
them give up

fall ravenous upon a canyon, reveal
its smoking naked contours

imbue with your stink the fur of the cat

extinguish dwelling places

just go ahead, you
and your nasty little freaky friend
the wind

Special effects ordered up by Mars
who sits by the pool with maidens either side
buffing his nails in bikinis

we'll do the rooflines aglow
he tells a sycophant
we'll do the totally vaporized

☙

We shouldn't be living here
anyway. At night
coyotes howl with laughter
and desire. Mars
is more human.

His attributes ours, his
accoutrements also:
      pool
      chariot
      barbecue
      wrath

My woods are charred
bituminous

black bark bleeds
red resin plasma

between the standing
broiled branchless poles

new unwelcome views of the lake

and of shocked humps of hills
self-conscious and sad, evicted

from their leafy life

naked rock, empty scorched treetops

where for weeks no bird had
or now would

ever sing

And now once more
the wind is blowing
and the fire surges
upon the town
and the countryside

the dear historic

what was lovely

the firs and the pines

the brown rabbit hopping

the canyon road to the railway trestles
where we took our brother and our mother
on a Sunday or a Wednesday
with its tall ears standing up

I would comfort if I could
but would have to wrestle it down

and feel its scared heart pounding

A stubble of blackened shards
where magpies fly, try
to settle – in autumn light

pine sap looks blue
against bark's carbonic crust

and a spray of brown needles
on the forest floor we pretend

are a carpet of grasses
and not a scorch of tears

upon the miles of roots that smoulder
still in molten maze

where a bluish haze appears to mark

the transit of ghosts and giants
who left an arsonist's hoard heaped

extinct matchsticks leaning
tip to tip

THE GOOD BACTERIA

1.

They had a view of the twinkling city as they ate.
Car lights were a ribbon along the shape of the bridge.
No one was there; all were ghosts in coats.

No more bloody ghazals! one ghost shouted to another.
In the morning they ate again, and took their penicillin pills.
The penicillin killed the good bacteria as well as the bad.

It killed all the bacteria, good and bad, like death or God.
Though death, being a matter of bacteria, is also life.
It was easier to walk to Kamloops.

He lugged his own laptop; it was easier that way.
On his lap sat the known universe.
When he sat down, the known universe sat on his lap.

He could see anything that way on the way to Kamloops.
A known ghost. The trees burned all the way to the sky.
His stomach burned when he took the penicillin.

2.

She pressed upon the part of her mind
that was titanium, Queen of the Fairies.

Lighter than air almost she was wringing salt
out where she'd wept into her hair.

Perched on a pear
leaf leaning out to see
insect heraldry. And to call
for a change in government.

With subtle blush and translucent
garments at 3 a.m. calling the cat away
from mouse ribs lest coyotes
with licked chops sneak up and pounce

like the government upon the night shift
poor and tired.

3.

A white lake gull grabbed a breeze.
Me and my sister were lying on the rocky beach.

A duck went swimming by, really hauling.
Seeing my sister he married her and she married him.
Down they went to an underwater house
whose chimney comes out where
the smoke bush grows.

Beside the smoke bush the electricity inspector
peers at a gauge on the house wall and writes
in his book.

My sister comes up for air and shakes herself
somewhat dry although her rump – so quick
to propel her downward to her happy home –
leaves a damp imprint on the car seat.

We poke at buttons on the dash until we get
some music we like. Another button and
the windows go down. Hand out, fingers
spread playing the warm currents of Peachland.

4.

As if we loved not only each other
but the weather we were happy
when the hummingbirds came
with suggestive beaks to the nectar-laden
honeysuckle and hovered shimmering like
someone wrote, *a winged mouse.* It was in
a not-nice book, especially the part
where the blameless woman's heart was broken.

They'd met for the first time at a clinic
with a terrible insect bite that would not go down.

After that they were inseparable. The book –
a novel – was set in the Arizona desert where no
apparent difference obtained between
life and death, taxidermy came up often
as a metaphor or a simile, a smile

often lurking on its countenance.

5.

A woman with the face of a sheepdog
or a sheepdog with the face of a woman
was sitting beside the driver – a young
Caucasian male – of a black F-150 pickup truck
speeding south on South Ridge Drive.

Anubis, Anubis, what a heck of a proboscis!

Later, a heart-rending bawling as of a goat
led to the slaughter echoed among the monster houses.

6.

Small round islands crammed with tall trees,
toupees of underwater giants. On balder crowns
eagles rest hooded and quiet, hangmen
at lunchtime.

Always losing wives. They disappear through
pinholes in the bottom of the ocean. They belong
to the goose world. Honking and hollering,
their divine soft breasts and missing children
sitting on a seat on an airplane. All the crying
and the carrying on, agencies like you wouldn't
believe, all helpless. Infinite worlds.

7.

In this life it has not been given me
to see that many bears.

One by the Hope-Princeton Highway.
One by the road up near Masset.
Another when a kid in Banff
where they wandered among the cars.

One on a hillside near some horses grazing
but it could have been a scarecrow
dark silhouette constructed of plywood
and erected in a bad mood
to discourage swans & other
beautiful things from landing and settling
with wide wings from elsewhere.

8.

I saw him coming down the street in the sunshine
eating an apple he'd bought at the grocery store.
The sea, the sea
glinted and humped behind him
devoid of any but anchored boats

his own waited in a tree
and had the face of a woman
he'd married once in a dream –

thereafter she carried him
on her back until the dream ended.

An orange popsicle was softening
in the grocery bag. While he sat in the café
among other songless birds
it melted, then liquefied, then vanished.

9.

And still the government remained the same
or worse. And what was frozen resumed.

And others fainted and fell to the ground.
Thinking themselves joined to the ineffable
with rubber bands and with foreknowledge,
so they could faint and fall, faint and fall
all day if they wanted.

Still the traffic twinkled on the bridge
and the lights of the dwellings along the shore
and higher up in the mountains twinkled
also as soon as night fell and all night
until morning the measure of those who forgot to turn out
their front porch light would be taken
by the electricity inspector.

Dials and gauges tremble with information,
the smoke bush sends out a new red shoot.

Quickly the sun rises like a big monster.
The moon is vanquished unlike ignorance
unlike getting it all wrong unlike we did it to ourselves.

10.

Across the hills and valleys
hurrying as if excited to have
found a dollar bill.

They had something to tell.
They concealed redness.

They humped over and in between.
They were infinite in number
leading up to the last one.

Circlets of blossom crown sleek heads
in the Olympic-size pool which quickly
are gone. The surface is silent.

Then erupts with smiles. Ducks
quack in the current of the stream
so bright they look painted.

On a treetop an eagle
devours a dead crow and black feathers
are drifting down.

The dead crow's best friend sobs nearby.
Everything moving and dropping.

11.

Under the scabbard and cover of night
Entrances islanded. Here in this furnished decor
Potholders are suspended from a daisy.

Complicated crosses with crooks.
And knots. Knotted and beguiled.
A swag of painted cherries like wounds lined up.

Circlets of roses, circlets of roses with ribbons.
Picture of three fishing boats two tall one small
Between them, their reflections waver.

The subject is elusive, like Artemis.
In those woods she shines but not here
In the house where all is pinkish.

Enter a real guy in a pleated skirt with a sword
Sunk in a scabbard, ten oxen
Couldn't drag him away from fighting.

Inside his myth he's very busy too.
Polishing his scabbard with Silvo, staunching
His cuts and abrasions he goes through tubes of Polysporin.

12.

There was a lot of waiting along the road.
Her brother sat in a truck all day waiting like this.
He saw some smoke then some helicopters
And airplanes casting orange smoke.

It was lunchtime just before the sawdust pile
Ignited from within. It was just like a movie
Or a corpse. Many corpses had been found
Under cars and on the road and in the market.

Pale-winged hawks hunted mice at the top.
They cast wide circles.
Even the dog looked like a cat at a mousehole
Digging and digging and staring stock-still.

The mice and the fires had a field day.
Me and my brother walked for a while
On the road that had no cars, that stayed
Between pines and tall white plants and purple ones.

Already we could hear the sound of the traffic.
Traffic and houses made of wood with maple cabinets,
An island kitchen, and killer ensuite.
In the dream we had, a mountain fell down.

I was calling the name of my son.

Interspersal 7

THE CELEBRATION

Was it a poorly attended event, a celebration
no one felt like celebrating? Was there no
live music? Was there
a table with small empanadas
and cubes of cheese, another with bottles of wine?
Had the winter day subsided into early
evening before the rush hour, white wine
larking in your bloodstream as you
walk to the parking lot? The prawns
had been large and plump, sweet.
Could you have eaten a dozen?
And besides, it turned out
that so-and-so had been born in
a small Eurasian town. Which of the following
instruments were generally played by popular persons?
(a)   accordion
(b)   banjo
(c)   piano

Was crockery flung at the mantel? Did they dance
with throats proud and uplifted?

Were they enjoined to celebrate some government policy or other?
Daycare day, eat broccoli day, safety day! Apology day! Not worrying
about anything day! Old guys driving vintage cars in the slow lane!
Young guys at the Keg on a big night out! Catholics playing six
cards each at the bingo hall! Insomniacs fretting with chamomile in
the kitchen! Old men weeping in the parks! Boys sobbing in armies!
Moloch, Moloch, celebration in Moloch! Travellers picking at room-
service chicken pot pies!
Underpaid clerks helpful at the insurance office! Hermaphrodite
trout! Box stores with irritable cashiers! Pepsi salesmen analyzing flow
charts! Grandmas eyeing the sherry! Orangutans grieving in zoos!

Secretaries! Undertakers!
Robots on the telephone! Oral hygienists! English professors defeated
by *poésie*! Celebrate! Celebrate!

The moon keeps me company all the way home, her dark smile and
brocade blouse.
We see her coming over the hills and duck into
the collar of our coat. We know perfectly well we could use a little
of her scorn, her glamour.

Weeping Willow

———

Radio New France Radio

WEEPING WILLOW

for Angela Bowering

The willow tree in winter,
skiff of snow on a wooden bench
placed thoughtful beneath
her boughs –

she'd had wing chairs
specially upholstered –

conversation's nexus –

two of them, the two of us,
our two cigarettes and another

voice going round on the record player
or emanating from a book

swish of traffic outside, her frequent
use of the word *absolutely*

Down Larch St. to suppertime.

Angela'd had another dream
in which a school of fish ...

& how she should have run off
with the visiting professor ...

– Dear reader,
shouldn't we all have run off with someone.

At any rate
we'd talked for hours at the kitchen table,
Angela dispensing Sweet'n Low
into her coffee as the windows darkened
and it was time to go so

I put on my coat and drove
down the hill in the Honda

many autumns back then

Weeping willow's lanky tresses
hide a bower, an ear

here, the long grass sere in autumn
reminds me of her yellow hair

long and swinging, sleek
when she searched for her lighter –

George you fucking asshole she would say
in the kitchen in her beautiful coat

We scuffed new boots in Seattle parking lots
& wore them home across the border.

Salespeople at Nordstrom back and forth
like a crazy dame movie
with stacks of shoeboxes tottering.
Always it seemed

she was at the bank, moving accounts around,
piling up interest –

Furniture arrived in truckloads, a fountain
splashed 'neath newly installed
Moorish mullioned windows beyond which
a lime-tree bower
her prison –

or so we joked and cackled –

In memory, murmurs, deep
Venusian glow of her topaz ring

Angela and I reviewing
some recent event uneventful really
to the naked eye. The topaz ring
slipping sideways on her paperwhite finger,
hand to mouth, hand to mouth, it was
the *J'accuse* of the student questionnaires –

That Thomas Hardy was way too hard.
That she would arrive late or eat a muffin
or go on and on.

We drank Piesporter
& I went to her dentist –
the very one who was on call
whenever the Queen was in town

& by then she was happy in her garden
just like the Queen, seed catalogues
stacked on the table her new
inamoratas roots and branches, rare

or uncommon and common as well,
beloved, poetry a balustrade
in all the rooms indoors and out

Arrayed in the plentiful hues
of the fashion then
and also now but then
we seldom took a walk

& the longer it's been
the younger we become

the two of us in a kitchen
our children in the next room
playing and murmuring

– *primitive philosophers*
she would say

tears welling

As she lay dying amidst the willow-pattern walls
a gardener pruned a Moorish vista from a row of trees

and the church across the street gonged with weddings
and with funerals, or the ordinary Sundays with the old
faithful getting out of cars and opening umbrellas

and wings of angels began to fill the room
palpable and crowding out physiology,
husband, daughter

the stack of mysteries on the bed

Reading a novel called *Being Dead*
and how windy and cold it is
in the everlasting hills.

I wish Angela were here.

We would talk and what we
talked about would knit together
a garment

in the willow bower where she sheltered
her unmendable body

Willow tree – fortress
and boudoir, rehab
of the mind-body split

Angela, I say,
I can't write love poems.

That's all right, she says.

Thinking pours from her hair,
head-to-toe silk on the way to her car,
white cigarette in ivory holder
clenched to one side
when she reached back into coat arms –

perfume floating, rainy day, time to go

RADIO NEW FRANCE RADIO

for Robin Blaser

<>

Now only the imagination
carries forward. Down those streets.
I didn't recognize
anybody. Until much later
& then only the daily merchants.
In an unexpected window
a displacement of memory –
you do not belong here or
you belong elsewhere

& I see your hands
different now
folding a newspaper around
then pausing over a coffee spoon
preoccupied, at rest. O the world
composes us strangers –

\<\>

Each tree in the park
is a Christmas tree, lit up
with ten-foot striped candy canes
and giant red and blue baubles,
and a few skaters out of Impressionism
carve up the frozen pathway
circling the fountain, the statue,
the boarded-up concession stand
beneath the stars & the luminous candy canes
sweetening the light that faces
rue Prince-Arthur.

\<\>

Tracks in the ice
the icy
heart can't stand
fear of slippage – the mind's
& falling down
in front of everyone

(Even with a broken leg
 I'd feel only a nuisance
 to the traffic)

There is no peace
in the quiet
the comings and goings
of the traffic or the human
soaring we hear as the song
on the radio, Victoria de los Ángeles
& the violins of the French orchestra

Similes of birds' flight
our awkward limbs tracing arcs
in the frozen
multitudinous *ayre* –

<>

The sky over the bus station
is mustard yellow
& greasy, 4 p.m. a Sunday
afternoon in March.
I was happy to be carrying
my red suitcase again
walking up rue Saint-Denis
on my own two feet.
One wonders about women
who have come away alone
from a bus station
& carry their own suitcase.
Unseemly, as if a cab driver
should be putting it in the trunk
while she settles herself
in the back seat, snapping open
a powder compact
to check her teeth and hair
crossing silky knees
and lighting up a Belvedere.
I didn't have far to go
only three blocks, a little dizzy
from the diesel air &
tired, not from walking alone
with my suitcase
but with an embarrassment
as old as history –
the desire to explain
to that grinning punk
in the black Mustang
that this is what I chose.

<>

At the typewriter
thinking something up
while the Saturday night cabs
honk & sidle up & down
the snowy streets.

I should probably be in one
all dolled up
in a midnight-blue sequined gown
but the air in this place!
so crackling and dry –
too many more sparks
& the whole town
could go up in flames.

<>

      Here the days
are grey & white and the nights
yellow & black
& there is no sunset only twilight
all the romance indoors
all the scenery human

      Pigeons guttural & iridescent
in the eaves built to imitate
a remembered vision of Normandy castle
grey stone, curving out
but regular & low

      On Sunday nights
the walls adjacent to the dance studio
shake with yelling flamenco dancers
stomping & clapping
in that quick urgent way, my face wavers
in the mirror when they practise
their *duende*

      Last night at 2:30 after watching
The Great Gatsby I thought
I heard a shot then screams
from the restaurant down below
oh no not the FLQ again
referendum fever running high &
always some nut with a gun

      but it must have been the wind
      or *The Great Gatsby*

     Even the sky
looks like a 1955 Social Studies textbook
old & Atlantic
carrying bits of Nova Scotian
ocean, the dust of Acadia.

<>

On Saturday mornings we meet to talk
women and poetry in the heated air
the charming song of the chanteuse mocks
unwilling our heavy coats and voices bare
that wish to say the things we daren't say –
draped in fur but not in Paris, no rouged lips
or horny sailors nor poets freshly off the ships
o'erwhelmed by this our beauty that will slay
them suddenly – oh no, this place is snowy
where grey days break through paler grey
and yonder waitress moves quite slowly
encumbered by necessity. O sanctuary brave
wherein we think our little hymns to Artemis
no unencumbered song, no earthly heaven this.

<>

Take my winter clothes
to the Fort Net
with the big *OUI* sign on it.
Students in black overcoats
& serious eyeglasses
gaze at waterfalls of dryers
or read *Le Devoir*, Jimmy Carter
on the use of force
& madame must charge me
quatre dollars pour la jupe.
It has a lining
probably nylon or polyester,
some petroleum derivative
whence also the fumy fluids
of her trade. These days
when spring is still a killed thing
& the wind is full of dust
the new world gets tough
on the old
& everyone looks grim
& pays through the nose
à travers des becs.

<>

Wending my way home, the unfamiliar
streets, the air not
like a song. Caught
outside the Faubourg Saint-Denis
by a street clown's awkward act –
throws three balls up in the air
& misses the catch, a boring routine.
His red cap on the sidewalk
for coins, small bills, Métro tickets.
No one laughs, the spectators
gaze dreamily out the steamed-up windows
& foggy foolish
breath emits steadily
like a locomotive
bearing down
from the distant, beige hills –
the unbroken blue western sky I fancy
it disappears into

<>

Montréal is no place
for optical illusions, no mountains
to dislodge themselves
to walk among us
advancing and retreating
with each breath taken in or given out
to the soft & bluish air.

Under that western sky
stalked by mountains
tracked by benign & rusty freighters
bitten by blossoms extravagant
& common, the walkers will find a place
by the water to sit for a minute
looking out. The world
turns to scenery again
and things hold still.

Interspersal 8

OH, HELLO COUNT, HOW ARE YOU, DO COME IN

The time and the car have to go. The light has to fall
in a beam from a cloud. The pebbles will rankle.
A stone is a mountain, a mountain a stone.
Sand is carted away. Ants cart a corpse. The hourglass
of their home is a sand volcano. Cobwebs
make hankies on the shrubbery. The clothes-
line sagging with pyjamas under the mad extravagance
of a high double rainbow, now in the photo album.
Is it mica and marble that streak the granite? The Count
loves Gertrude but Gertrude loves Tim. Is it true
we desire desire? Alas
we are the Count, ever hopeful at the door
of immortality like car bombers. I think I ruined those roses,
the ones the deer didn't eat. Sway of tall trees nevertheless
at the edges of the yard each and every
exploding autumn.

A Holy Experiment

———

The Nets of Being

———

The Consumptives
at Tranquille
Sanatorium, 1953

———

At My Mother's in
Prince George

A HOLY EXPERIMENT

for Frances Motz Boldereff

1. *Jerry Geiger was Boldereff's friend in Woodward, Pennsylvania, many
   years ago.*

One night, her friend Jerry had her look at the sky through his telescope.
"That's the MOON?" Frances said. It was sometime in the
mid-to-late 1950s, "La Motz" was one of her *noms de plume.*

After her funeral and at the small
gathering afterwards, Jerry talked
about the massive heavy presses made of ancient
wood and stone that every autumn
were used to press the apple cider.

The icy cold cider lay in tanks in the earth. Any
sort of jar with a lid stored it –
pickle jars, mayonnaise jars. While visiting Jerry
the next day we had a glass or two each.

Up in the watchtower where he once
kept his telescope we ascended narrow stairs,
looked out as if we were Frances that long-ago night,
came back down the steep stairway with serious faces,
a wooden stairway more like a ladder.

Not far, over some mountains, the current of the Susquehanna River
pouring, the beautiful word "Susquehanna" new to my tongue.

We said goodbye beside the rental car in the rain. Along the path,
fierce little mottled apples strewn by the wind and at the cemetery
the ashes of Frances beneath a fresh pile of dirt in the family
plot, a dozen granite headstones all saying MOTZ.

2. *In worn-out chairs, we sat in his kitchen.*

Rows and jars of homemade reddish-brown &
dark-green medicines gathered from the
plush land at the end of the road. The world was different
and quite what I guess I would call "American."

He had asked Frances to look at the moon through his telescope.
The night must have been clear and black, the moon
bright and full. What did she see: a bunch of
shadows, crags and valleys, craters full of
darkness. Were they lovers, we were dying to ask. Whatever,
he had a doctorate in the metaphysics of spirals.

That shut us up for a while.

He must have brought her over from Woodward
in his car to view the moon. She had already named him
president of her five-book publishing company,
where every cent poured, to which she sacrificed
the rent and went for years without a decent hairbrush.

3. *For this ailment, for that, he had a cure.*

He could have been a soldier
in the last years of the war
or come of age around the time I was born.

Maybe this has to do with the weirdness
and warp of time, the spiralling going nowhere.
One is neither here nor there
and doesn't know what to say.

One sits in the perished chair and listens.
Like a bending of the rain the thought of William Penn,
said to have been fair and wise
which is why the Susquehannock trusted him.
Attractive, clear-eyed, idealistic –
this charisma led them all to *a holy experiment.*

Science magazines in stacks
on the kitchen table, radio antennae
at several different angles conspire in the ether.

4. *We were staying at an old, old inn.*

What if something supernatural happened?
Floors sloped, ornate would be the preferred
decor of such a place, visited by tourists,
mourners, certain parties of folks.

The rain fell heavily on the Susquehanna River
and on the Susquehannock and the Germans
in their graves, if they had them
and didn't just die in the woods with an antique
rifle or a hatchet in their hands.

And almost like those dead I slept
and forgot my tickets and passport

So I had to return
to the little house
and ask to use the phone
which ruins everything
since you've said goodbye, you're
in the past, and now
you're back.

They dial for you if you can't find your glasses
right away. And when you leave for the second time
let's all hope it will be the last.

5. *Expressways and turnpikes, off-ramps, antacid vapour lights.*

The Susquehanna would reveal
what lay around the bend in the beauty and the silence –
the silence of nature, not silent at all.

In her nighttime I wandered afresh with
the map obscure by my side,
a rough map the size of a placemat. So many roads
so little time! I tore along in the purple Galant
looking for turnoffs, slowed on village streets, places
crowded close to the road like Aaronsburg,
Jerry's place not far from there where hills
and woods began.

Farmland all around, farms out of a story-
book hugely romanticized. Mennonite,
Amish, or just plain Yanks wearing rain jackets and
opening doors. Any autumn afternoon was sepia toned
and frightened, like a commercial for insurance.

Long ago of course this was all moot or a moat.
Motz built Woodward and Frances who like a deity
had many names and situations sacred to her ups and downs

returned to be a MOTZ in the cemetery across the road
from her library, her parlour.

THE NETS OF BEING

Awake, my sleeping ones, I cry out to you,
disentangle the nets of being!
 —Charles Olson

The net can be very dangerous.
 —Tito Gaona
  Aerialist, Ringling Brothers Circus

An array of hairnets – the hairnets of Jove's wife
& those who work in the kitchens of Jove

placing feet on filament horizontals
climbing *each step of the ladders*

into the firmament
along the length of a sunset's horizon

in the space of the Big Top
one makes a catch, another, the throw

the grip, brother to brother, was phenomenal,
for the triple mid-air somersault

he climbed the twenty-one Lucite rungs
of the slender rope ladder with an aerialist's

sideways climb, each slippered foot placed
around a side rope onto a rung

his brother already waiting
hanging upside down

the feat applauded by janitors and clowns
the afternoon of rehearsal, each knot

of the net below its own particular fire
welding the wounds of separation
as smudges of the dead return grabbing

the instants which were not lived

#s of sunrises, #s of people and
personality types going to work in the kitchens

and sweatshops of cosmos stitching
fast the seams of flailing garments

flung down towards the next
step in the track of making,
each dangling thread

particular as the leavings of a beard in the sink,
pennants of DNA in the slight moons of clipped nails

stray strands tucked into the shower caps of the kids
making computers and cellphones
in moon suits, the moon's white bone

catches the reflection of tossed pebbles
the corner of a floating net, a knot
untying, a stray strand escaping,

hyacinth sunrise of the fire opal a far-off vent
of breath & peace carved out from

the mammothness of the comings & goings
of the ladders of life

#

one had her hair plaited
to the harness she hung from

to avoid the burn of the nets
below *which could really hurt*

she juggled flaming torches
she did multiple rapid body spins

one day her hair unknotted
and she fell to the tanbark, having said
no net I am fastened by my hair
to the air

and broke her neck but lived

the nets which entangle us are flames
spread out across each plane of being

#

back in some *histoire d'amour*
a pair of laddered stockings is laid aside

a world is coloured
by jars of licorice, banded pigeons, soft-hued parasols

firefly sparks and embroidery hoops
stitched to sadness by a stray song

winter furs so cold the various pellicles stand out
like the faint beard of a Viking woman

#s of iron filings hopelessly in love
with a toy magnet, a tilted globe spinning to indicate

the magnificent travel plans of railway plutocrats
puffed up in furs and feathers

alighting in foreign lands to fezzes and muezzins
camels kneeling and rising laden with women

insomniacs, black circles under their eyes,
dead souls, some record playing on the Victrola,

silhouettes, flakes of poppy, tassels
softly sweeping away a dream

#

black hair, blind dark, tantalizing tangle
of flecks and #s of luminous horizons

take your pick: the pebble, the funnel, the nest,
the vitreous floater beneath frosted-blue eyeshadow

the Black Hole or the oval sky-blue vent
the stitched, the laced, the #s of gems, the debris

of ourselves, flakes and lashes, rashes
caught in the trammels, *the multiple nets*

#

slender beings laced into sparking spangles ascend, descend

one the flyer, one the catcher, one
spins by the hair juggling flaming torches

another below, lancing a blister with a heated hatpin,
the unguent warm spread of its water across

the palm of the hand that had gripped the bar
in the spotlight dark of the Big Top

as angels and demons and men
go up and down

two horses run around with one rider straddling both
two clowns drive a tiny car at top speed honking

what wind clears the sodden weights of goods & equipment
let none of the threads be left upon the earth

let there be only paradise

#

going to get our stitches out, following grids
of streets and traffic, appointments, #s of duties

we examine the new scar's border of threads
& unravel filaments of time, #s of memories

bunched up in nerve fibres clinging together
like the rubber tires which in Olson's dream

looked as though they only needed air,
the rear tires *masses of rubber & thread*

clear dawning breaks through the deep bruise of night
a remnant of mesh floats away on the breeze

\#

bone-coloured cloud, sparks from the campfire,
beach pebbles laid out as discrete thoughts

as sun goes down and stars come up
a dark train speeds along black tracks

the black tracks are left hot
the opal moon rises

a mesh of static spread out,
Andromeda ticking and whooshing

like the bloodstream, inconstant,
melodic, secret –

antennae tweaked to cosmos
where the threads of life are snipped

and left in tiny piles as below the chair of the barber
the brunette leavings of the customer now paying

lie, and the customer among #s of customers
returns to work, dons a hairnet,

shoves down into the deep fryer the mesh pan
cold bone-white shards criss-cross

arrayed like martyrs in vegetable surrender
to the nets we are entangled in

\#

sparks of stars in space debris
subducted bonfires of the actual

the nets which entangle us are flames
Olson writes, having looked up the Five Hindrances

under "Buddhism" in the *Encyclopedia Britannica,*
writing *to alleviate the dream*

writing to alleviate poetry, the mother, the beam
of the projector in the darkened living room

\#

the spotlight finds the catcher hanging upside down
not by his knees from the catch bar

but with the ropes that support the bar wrapped
tightly around his legs, *o souls, in life and in death*

catcher and flyer grip each other's wrists
and hold on tight

and that's when the janitors and clowns
came racing out shouting and clapping

the night in Tucson Miguel Vázquez
turned over four times in mid-air

into the hands of his brother Juan
at just that moment before I really start to fall

he said, *I float there for a second
and my brother caught me at just that moment*

#

threaded filaments through
the eye of cosmic sewing

stitching the wounds of separation
knitting a nexus of filaments, nests, nets

a knot loosened, an end dangling
pulled through history

a woman sewing a button on a cuff
breaks the thread with her teeth

young girls stitch furiously in factories
in textile dust 24-7 opalescent fabrics

mauve, orange, azure-blue
sunrise a memory, #s of black patterns

strewn like the petals of a starburst
and you wonder, do they think

the fabrics are beautiful, do they crave them
as what slides through their authentic hands

is a mauveness matching the circles under their eyes
                              or an azure blue the colour of eternal rest.

THE CONSUMPTIVES AT TRANQUILLE
SANATORIUM, 1953

Gaunt hills
pine-dotted are the view
beyond the books propped
against the sun on the blanketed
laps of consumptives
taking the air.
Wild horses,
black cattle
cast shadows the
size of flies. Moving down
to winter shelter.

$\diamond$
$\diamond$

Bright blood startles white pans.
By green pastures,
the still waters, lambs of Jesus
rescued from tree limbs and
lightning. White beds,
white nurses, white
cream by the cupful.

◇
◇

Flies and hornets sidle against the screens
of verandas in the afternoon. Haze
and heat, doze and fever shudder. The book
falls to the lap. Across the lake, a horse
rubs against the soothing roughness
of a pine, releasing resin, retsina, plangent
wine of rebetiko singers themselves
exiled and sometimes between acts
feverish on a shabby divan.

◇
◇

It's as quiet as the skin on a custard.
Gardeners slip and prune and feed.
Gladiolas' leek-like straight strong stalks
a reproach. The consumptives –
delicate, sensitive – victims of cities,
bad air, bad drains, bad
fiction, hard lives, a lack
of sunshine and morals.

◇
◇

Best they be housed far out of town
where their spit won't dry into dust
and then be blown into innocent
eyes and mouths when it gets hot out
& the wind leaps from side streets.

◇
◇

Some of the nurses are not very happy.
Perhaps, not the cream of the crop? Forced
to these purposes: must have been forced –
or punished.
And disapproving of consumption,
though a charitable
intent to some degree could redeem
the situation. If a leper colony was
martyrdom, at least it was far away,
and had overtones.

◊

In the heat of the afternoon, in the cold,
year after year the consumptives are wheeled out
to rest, to read on the veranda. And snooze
and doze. With double blankets and a hat
and red and seeping nose.

◊

Early summer, fresh air flexing muscle.
Season of buttercups, green lawns,
tender vistas. A few cars coming in, going out.
On Sundays, children: some quiet, some confused
as they gather for photos in the Sunken Garden.

◊

A small crinkle-edge photo shows us
dressed up by a flowering shrub

– not recalling what I felt then, since my mother
being there had been gone and was still there &
gone.

◇
◇

Her dark hair grew longer. Her young life
grew older. I learned to read. I drew birds
in Art.

◇
◇

An array of consumptives, male and female,
young, old, Indigenous from the "Queen Charlottes"
or up north, or dank Vancouver, or the War.
Nurses shook down thermometers, served
cupfuls of heavy cream and plenty of
eggs, eggs to the point of choking, also the cream.

◇
◇

Life was tranquil.
Effort discouraged. Patients gazed at the everlasting hills,
where cattle dispersed & returned.
Doctors, nurses, coroners, visitors
with lilac branches and gloves on, fear
of death palpable in the heat of the day,
the perfect climate, *better than Egypt* brayed
the local boosters.

Heat & radiation treatments shimmered
the lungs of the dying and the not-so-dead, a torrid dryness
camels could have plodded through,
saddles jingling with tambourines and laden with the rubies
of pomegranates, the oasis
where they kneel, where they are disburdened,
where they yawn and show their shocking teeth.

AT MY MOTHER'S IN PRINCE GEORGE

The river runs by so quietly
you'd fall into it if you were blind or daydreaming
its path so deeply scored

so unimpeded by rock or shoal
it fails to sing
or splash but only proceeds

in the one clear direction, south, I guess,
though it may at times diverge
as the bending valleys pull it onward

through canyons and underneath bridges
where a bright bush adorns a gravelly edge
people once sat on, thinking about something

as I do in my mother's guest room's
1940s honeymoon bedroom suite, thick maple
bedframe, dressing table with photos propped

on a beige linen runner.
Old brushes and combs.
A mirror with a long handle.

My mother and I watch TV,
eat our small supper

"You're so smart, dear," she says,
"you should be on *Jeopardy!*"

The winning contestant loses all her prize money
with a wrong answer but clearly
has learned the protocol:

No crying or whining!
No gloating either, when it's the other guy
standing there with nothing all of a sudden.

The new categories are revealed with a flourish.
We top up our glasses with Mom's homemade shiraz.
The three contestants look calm behind their pulpits.

Tonight's chamber concert is titled "Waning Crescent"
for the type of moon it is this night. Among other pieces
Mozart's "The Hunt" from the Haydn Quartets
will be performed at the Lutheran Church with
its austere altar & fine acoustics. The oboist is from Portugal.

It was beautiful but
driving around in the pitch dark afterwards
feeling old and diminished in capacities,
powerless and lonely in my mother's car

trying to read the street signs, pretending
I know where I'm going, the guy behind me
pushing with high beams on

near where big dim houses twinkle on a far hillside
way beyond my ken, I don't know this place anymore

and I got turned around exiting the Lutheran Church
parking lot where the outside lights weren't working and
a fellow with a flashlight was motioning this way, this way

It's nearing the end of hunting season.
Pickups have been through the car wash & sedans
contain more customers going to Seniors' Day at the pharmacy
than camouflage-clad customers
surveying the parking lot in their rear-view mirrors.

Inside the pharmacy, swift and busy dispensing of tablets
and instructions.

When my name is called I rise with alacrity.
I can hear all right, I can get out of here,
just an errand for my mother, not me, not yet.

The concertmaster announced that Mozart's "The Hunt"
wasn't really about a hunt. It was just the name it
ended up with because of the prominence of horns.
I'm not alone, though I'm alone here.
I worry about my mother, who is 90 and having trouble.
One of us should move up here for a while.
I think of all those I know with faraway mothers –
one in South Africa, several in England. Prince George
isn't that far but by now, my carry-on
is bulging and heavy, zipped up, the handle extended.

A huntress kneels in the night sky
drawing an arrow from her quiver. A carved wooden bear
is standing up
at the Arrivals entrance at the airport looking like a man
in a bear suit, which is what a bear is
in the occlusion of the waning crescent –
truth so modestly, so hilariously hidden
and present in the painted fur and long claws
of our disguises. The shuttle arrives at 4:40 a.m.,
stars still out, the other passengers
mute shapes looking out the window
at nothing, the odd building with lights on,
or just darkness going by, already gone.

Interspersal 9

IN THE CAR WASH

In the car wash
water-feathers swoop and sweep
then splats of blue stuff,
then splats of pink stuff,
then the going-over with the protectant –
then the whumping of the dryers
scattering sideways froth & bubbles
as if parting the sheer curtain that divides us

& in the car wash's various illuminations
and showerings from up above & sideways
I'm reading Thomas Merton's little chapter
on "Silence" ... opened at random – and "Silence"
isn't about silence at all but about nature.

When the great door lifts and the light goes green
we emerge – my car, my self, & the thoughts of Thomas Merton –
into an alley with winter weeds and branches
pressing hard against a fence as each clean car appears
with its happy occupant, its shining force.

Care for the Plenitude of the World

Sharon and I had many conversations during the editing of *Refabulations*, and she wanted to let readers eavesdrop on us, suggesting we do an interview as her afterword. On reading her answers to my questions, I suggested that we remove my words and let hers stand, organized by subject, so that readers can hear Sharon speak. Most of the subjects she covers could be filed under "living a life in poetry." But I stole her words to call it "Care for the Plenitude of the World."

—Erín M.

ST ON COLLABORATION

I was born left-handed under the sign of partnerships, and my life has been full of partnerships and collaborations, including this one with Erín. *The Wig-Maker* came out of a conversation with, and then a commitment to, a neighbour, Janet Gallant, who told me she had a story to tell. She talked; I typed. My job was first to listen, then to organize her sentences into a narrative, and then to explain, in an afterword, what had happened during that process. Among other notable collaborations, I slowly worked with Ralph Maud over decades to edit and transcribe Charles Olson's correspondence with book designer Frances Boldereff, which came out in two volumes (the first published by Wesleyan University Press in the US in 1999 and the second by Talonbooks in 2012 under Greg Gibson's editorship). On top of writing dozens of blurbs of poetry books and anthologies, I hosted Pinecone Poetry Workshops at my home for a few years post retirement from UBC Okanagan – with the assistance of my husband, Paul, and a neighbour friend, Diane Callbeck, who handled administration. Part of a recent documentary film by Curtis Emde, *Why We Write: Poets of Vernon*, about the North Okanagan writing community, was filmed during one of these workshops. Hannah Calder, who collaborated on the film, is a former creative-writing student of mine at Capilano College, and has since published a novel with New Star Books, a press that has published me and poets I've admired and written about, like George Stanley and Barry McKinnon and Lisa Robertson. These circulations of creative and poetic energy and imagination are, to me, the essence of what "community" and "collaboration" mean.

ON EDITING AND ITS ROLE IN COMMUNITY

It wouldn't have occurred to me to publish my own work in *TCR* when I was poetry editor in the late 1970s and editor from 2001 to 2005, let alone in either edition of *The New Long Poem Anthology*, or in *LAKE: A Journal of Arts and Environment*, which I co-edited later on with poet Nancy Holmes at UBC Okanagan, I mean from an ethical standpoint. *TCR* has published my work since then, though, including *The Sharon Thesen Issue* (2008) edited by Jenny Penberthy. I reread, on the occasion of his passing a few months ago, my first husband Brian Fawcett's piece in that issue, titled "Why Sharon Thesen Doesn't Win Poetry Prizes." (In short, I'm a smart-ass.) Erín has her own stories about first reading *TCR* back in the late seventies, and I won't ever forget her first poetry submission to the *Review*. The connection between the Canadian and American avant-garde was strong then, already established in the TISH years in Vancouver. It was the defining spirit of my education at SFU in the late sixties, where I read Pound, Williams, Creeley, Duncan, Spicer, and Olson in undergraduate poetry classes. Some of those poets were still alive then. The alert reader will notice in this list the absence of women poets. However, Daphne Marlatt, the poetry editor at *TCR* just prior to me, had and has been a vital link maintaining the connections between UBC, SFU, so-called Black Mountain poetics, and the TISH poets, herself among them. The late Douglas Barbour and I used to joke about being half a generation younger than the TISH poets, and never being able to shake off our "junior" status.

ON CAMARADERIE

Interaction among Canadian poets in the seventies and eighties was a significant part of our writing and social lives. The Canada Council was generous, small presses were enthusiastic; wherever you lived, readings by out-of-town poets were happening all the time. Invite someone from Québec to read at a *TCR* event in North Vancouver? No problem! Having a book published in Toronto? No problem! You could fly out and back for the launch. We usually stayed at one another's houses, which meant after-parties and more talking and connecting. This camaraderie began to disperse when neoliberalism took a dimmer view of value-for-money when it came to arts funding, and the ascendancy of theory and M.F.A. programs began to break writers up into factions and silos of bureaucratic obsessions.

ON EDITING FOR YEARS BEFORE HER OWN FIRST BOOK

My first book, *Artemis Hates Romance,* made a splash when it came out in 1980. To some it seemed a late start, I suppose. But I'd stopped writing after marrying Brian in 1966 – he was the poet, I was the poet's wife, who had worked as a stenographer. We were going to Simon Fraser University together, both of us majoring in English. I typed his essays and my own essays. I also typed on stencil all the issues of *Iron* magazine we co-edited while we were undergraduates at SFU, students of Robin Blaser and Ralph Maud. The English Department let us use their Gestetner in the evenings to run the mimeographed issues off. We published work by Robin Blaser and Jack Spicer alongside Prince George poets like Brett Enemark, and art work for the covers was done by local artists such as Victoria Margesson and Renée Van Halm. We had a lot of American friends as well, students at SFU who were living in Canada because of the Vietnam War. This physical and immediate relation to contemporary poetry and exposure to it affected my line, my imagination, my sense of what poetry was supposed to be. Exercising editorial judgment, such as it was, was part of the adventure. *Iron* morphed into *NMFG* (No Money from the Government) after Brian and I split up in 1972. I stayed on at SFU and did my master's thesis on Coleridge's Shakespeare criticism, far from the ground – intellectual, social, aesthetic – I'd been covering as an undergraduate. My first independent and serious editorship was for a selected poems of Phyllis Webb. Her work had impressed me like no other up to that point. We worked together on *The Vision Tree*. I wrote an introduction, Talon published it, and it won the Governor General's Award for Poetry that year, 1982.

ON BEING A "RECEIVER"

The role of "the receiver" I believe I inherited from my father, who was a Morse-code telegrapher with CN, and previous to that, a code breaker for the navy in WW II. Morse code is nothing but listening, tapping, and rhythms. When I moved to Vancouver in 1964, I got a job at CKWX radio station working with a Dicta-phone machine. In my own work, I go by ear – sound, rhythm, line, the poem discovering something, finding itself, its spirit in language. As opposed to serving the already-spoken.

The retyping of decades of my own work, receiving my own work, for this book, is in a way an anxious doubling: the me now and the me then colliding on the page as the lines appear, as if the poem's composition is taking place in two time periods simultaneously. It's hard to believe how artful and often how awful the writing is, not to mention the time-warp disorientation of being taken back to old houses, old atmospheres, old feelings. At times I felt a motherly affection for that struggling young woman; at other times I was amused by her tough-guy persona, which I suppose was my idea of being a feminist at the time. How could anyone not be a feminist? But I chafed against "feminism" just as I chafed and still chafe against any "ism": categories and abstractions. I prefer to write and be "exempt from public haunt," as Shakespeare says in *As You Like It*.

ON A LIFE IN POETRY

Really that's the desire and it's what I live, what we share and where we can meet; a life in poetry, and not a "career" in it. Poets intent on a career don't seem to stray far from academia, I've observed, unlike the old-fashioned "famous poets," a category going extinct. Old-fashioned famous poets did not comply with the institutional, though many were articulate scholars and teachers, but they had a life in poetry too, by which I mean a life in which poetry is not instrumental but an essential way of experiencing life in community, conversation, conduct, work.

ON HER OWN TEACHING

What I most wanted to share or impart to others while teaching was care for the plenitude that the world is. To find their own particular way in this "everything," this "wild intelligence," this cosmos, which includes them.

ON BRITISH COLUMBIA, WHICH FILLS HER WORK

BC is an unstable geomancy of rock, trees, rivers, oceans, islands, fires, earthquakes, volcanos, floods, grasslands, and mountains, part of the bioregion "Cascadia" (in English), which extends southward as far as northern California. I often refer to myself as a Cascadian poet. For most of my life I've lived in the Cascadian bioregion and I have historic connections with the San Francisco Renaissance and other poets associated with Don Allen's *New American Poetry* (1960) anthology. I'm currently working with Paul Nelson and his Cascadia Poetics Lab, a hub of contemporary poetry and poetics based in Seattle, for whom I'll be editing a collection of interviews called *Cascadian Prophets*. The Okanagan Valley, the part of Cascadia where I live in BC, is at the northernmost tip of the Sonora Desert and is part of the Traditional Lands of the Syilx People. The English translation of the Ńsyilxčn' word for the Land, tmxʷulaxʷ, is "this braided spiral of time and living beings." That should be a sufficient poetics for anybody.

ON DEDICATION

I'm dedicating this book to Robin Blaser, teacher, guide, companion, friend, inspiration, godfather to my son, and pure magic in my life and art. And with feelings of deepest gratitude to Erín Moure, for helping bring this book to life, starting years ago in what we jokingly called our Kelowna "office," a sushi spot near the YLW airport halfway between our then houses, a spot where we have shared many a lunch and afternoon-long slow conversation about squid and lakes and books and poetry.

Acknowledgments

I am grateful to the editors of magazines, chapbooks, and anthologies who, over the years, have published some of the poems in this edition; as well as the original publishers and editors of the books these works were included in: Coach House Press, House of Anansi Press, Oolichan Books, McClelland & Stewart, Talonbooks, and New Star Books. I am particularly grateful to Erín Moure for her efforts and inspiration as editor, proofreader, consultant, and friend, and for the lively poetic intelligence she brought to this project. I'd also like to thank Catriona Strang for her conscientiousness and enthusiasm.

You don't write, teach, edit, and think about poetry for forty years without owing thanks to innumerable people, living and dead, near and far, in both life and art, in friendship, and in books, conversation, laughter, correspondence, collaboration, and inspiration. And I owe a debt of thanks too to my husband Paul, always.

Notes

The book's epigraph is from Etel Adnan, *Journey to Mount Tamalpais*, 2nd ed. (New York: Litmus Press, 2021).

The italicized lines that close "A Pair of Scissors, 13" are poetically borrowed from Ted Hughes's description of Proserpina in his *Tales from Ovid* (London: Faber & Faber, 1997). The epigraph to the poem is from Virginia Woolf, *Mrs Dalloway* (1925).

The Heraclitus quote that is epigraph to "The Occasions" was translated by Guy Davenport and is from *Herakleitos and Diogenes* (San Francisco: Grey Fox Press, 1979).

The italicized words that close the poem section on page 74 of "Gala Roses" are from Richard Grossinger, *Planet Medicine: Origins* (Berkeley, CA: North Atlantic Books, 1995), p. 37.

The Song of the Sibyl in "From Toledo" refers to a liturgical chant sung since early medieval times on Christmas Eve in northern Iberia and in the south of France and on Sardinia in Italy, in which the sibyl Eriythraea (from a text translated by Saint Augustine in *City of God* from a Greek acrostic poem) prophesizes the birth of Christ. The Council of Trent forbade it in 1563, but it was soon revived on Mallorca. The Mallorcan El Cant de la Sibil·la was declared a UNESCO Masterpiece of the Oral and Intangible Heritage of Humanity in 2010: ich.unesco.org/en/RL/chant-of-the-sybil-on-majorca-00360. Though once performed with boys as the sibyls, today the performers can be of any gender. The oldest surviving Spanish version of *The Song of the Sibyl* in the cathedral of Toledo was composed by Cristóbal de Morales.

"From Toledo" was published as a chapbook by Gorse Press (Barry McKinnon) in December 2007 in an edition of fifty for private distribution.

"Confabulations" echoes lines from Malcolm Lowry's fiction and letters. The Lowry epigraph that opens the poem is from volume 2, *1947–1957*, of *Sursum Corda! The Collected Letters of Malcolm Lowry*, ed. Sherrill E. Grace (Toronto: University of Toronto Press, 1996). The second epigraph is from Gaston Bachelard's 1938 book *La psychanalyse du feu*, translated as *The Psychoanalysis of Fire* by Alan C.M. Ross (Boston: Beacon Press, 1987). The Lowry poem quoted at the beginning of "Confabulations" is from *Selected Poems of Malcolm*

Lowry, ed. Earle Birney (San Francisco: City Lights Books, 1962). Elsewhere in the poem: the italicized lines on pages 112, 113, and 123 are from Malcolm Lowry's *Under the Volcano* and on page 118 from Lowry's story "The Forest Path to the Spring" in *Hear Us O Lord from Heaven Thy Dwelling Place: Stories*. Another source is Douglas Day's biography *Malcolm Lowry* (Oxford: Oxford University Press, 1973). Phrases taken directly from these sources are italicized, except where italics would produce an undesired emphasis. In all cases, images and situations have been lifted, spliced, and grafted where they were not just out-and-out invented. The poem is not intended to be a factual account of Malcolm Lowry's life.

The cadences in "The Good Bacteria" are inspired by Robert Bringhurst's retranslations (from the 1905 transcriptions and translations by John R. Swanton) of classical Haida literature in *A Story as Sharp as a Knife: The Classical Haida Mythtellers and Their World* (Vancouver: Douglas & McIntyre, 1999, and 2nd ed. 2011).

The epigraphs to "The Nets of Being" are from Charles Olson, "As the Dead Prey upon Us," in *The Distances: Poems by Charles Olson* (New York: Grove Press, 1960), and from *The American Circus: An Illustrated History,* by John Culhane (New York: Henry Holt, 1990). Both the Olson poem and the circus book lend their language at times (in italics) to the poem. Some of the imagery in "The Nets of Being" comes from a series of paintings by Marion Llewellyn called "Targeting Light Sources," first shown in West Vancouver at the Bellevue Gallery in 2009. Some of them can be seen at marionllewellynartist.com.

"In the Car Wash" and "At My Mother's in Prince George" first appeared in *The Receiver* (Vancouver: New Star Books, 2017) and are reprinted with kind permission of the publisher.

List of Original Publications

"A Holy Experiment," *The Good Bacteria*, 2006.

"A Pair of Scissors," *A Pair of Scissors*, 2000.

"After Roy Kiyooka's Funeral," *Aurora*, 1995.

"At My Mother's in Prince George," *The Receiver*, 2017.

"Being Adults," *The Beginning of the Long Dash*, 1987.

"The Beginning of the Long Dash," *The Beginning of the Long Dash*, 1987.

"Biography of a Woman," *Aurora*, 1995.

"The Celebration," *The Capilano Review* 3, no. 5 (Spring 2008).

"Clematis Montana Rubens," *A Pair of Scissors*, 2000.

"Confabulations," *Confabulations: Poems for Malcolm Lowry*, 1984.

"The Consumptives at Tranquille Sanatorium, 1953," *Oyama Pink Shale*, 2011.

"The Fire," *The Good Bacteria*, 2006.

"Five Preludes," *Oyama Pink Shale*, 2011.

"From Toledo" (chapbook), 2007.

"Gala Roses," *Aurora*, 1995.

"The Good Bacteria," *The Good Bacteria*, 2006.

"I Drive the Car," *Aurora*, 1995.

"In the Car Wash," *The Receiver*, 2017.

"The Nets of Being," *Oyama Pink Shale*, 2011.

"The Occasions," *The Beginning of the Long Dash*, 1987.

"Oh, Hello Count, How Are You, Do Come In," *The Good Bacteria*, 2006.

"The Parrot," *Aurora*, 1995.

"Parts of Speech," *Artemis Hates Romance*, 1980.

"Radio New France Radio," *Holding the Pose*, 1983.

"Six," *The Beginning of the Long Dash*, 1987.

"Skylarks," *The Good Bacteria*, 2006.

"The Watermelon," *Aurora*, 1995.

"Weeping Willow," *The Good Bacteria*, 2006.

Selected Bibliography

BOOKS
The Wig-Maker. Vancouver: New Star Books, 2021.
The Receiver. Vancouver: New Star Books, 2017.
Oyama Pink Shale. Toronto: House of Anansi Press, 2011.
The Good Bacteria. Toronto: House of Anansi Press, 2005.
A Pair of Scissors. Toronto: House of Anansi Press, 2000.
News & Smoke: Selected Poems. Vancouver: Talonbooks, 1999.
Aurora. Toronto: Coach House Press, 1995.
The Pangs of Sunday. Toronto: McClelland & Stewart, 1990.
The Beginning of the Long Dash. Toronto: Coach House Press, 1987.
Confabulations: Poems for Malcolm Lowry. Lantzville, BC: Oolichan Books, 1984.
Holding the Pose. Toronto: Coach House Press, 1983.
Artemis Hates Romance. Toronto: Coach House Press, 1980.

CHAPBOOKS
With Penn Kemp. *PS.* Toronto: Gap Riot Press, 2022.
With Marion Llewellyn. *The Nets of Being.* Vancouver: Dream Dead Press, 2009.
From Toledo. Prince George: Gorse Press, 2007.
Scrap Book. Edmonton: Olive Reading Series Collective, 2006.
Weeping Willow. Vancouver: Nomados, 2005.
Po-It-Tree: A Selection of Poems and Commentary. Burnaby, BC: Simon Fraser University, 1992.
Sheet Music. Burnaby, BC: Simon Fraser University, 1982.
Radio New France Radio. Vancouver: Slug Press, 1981.
The Imagination of Awakening: Endings of Some of Shakespeare's Comic Plays. Coquitlam, BC: T. Grieve and H. Hoekema, 1973.

BOOKS EDITED
With Ralph Maud. *After Completion: The Later Letters of Charles Olson and Frances Boldereff.* Vancouver: Talonbooks, 2012.
With Ralph Maud. *Charles Olson and Frances Boldereff: A Modern Correspondence.* Middletown, CT: Wesleyan University Press, 1991.
The New Long Poem Anthology. Coach House Press, 1991; 2nd ed: Talonbooks, 2001.
Webb, Phyllis. *The Vision Tree: Selected Poems of Phyllis Webb.* Vancouver: Talonbooks, 1982.

ESSAYS

"Olson & Love: The Transformative Correspondence with Frances Boldereff." Annual Charles Olson Lecture, Cape Anne Museum in conjunction with the Gloucester Writers' Center, Gloucester, MA (October 29, 2022). vimeo .com/756793608.

"Sharon Thesen." Poetry in Canada. Accessed July 2021. www.poetrycanada.org /digital-library-archive/sharon-thesen.

Introduction to *Waterloo Express*, by Paulette Jiles. Toronto: House of Anansi Press, 2nd ed., 2019.

"After-Thoughts on the Long Poem." Panel "Writing, Editing, and Publishing the Long Poem" at the League of Canadian Poets Annual General Meeting in Winnipeg, MB (May 30, 2015). www.malahatreview.ca/long_poem_papers /thesen.html.

"Rewilding Poetry." Panel "Rewilding Poetry" at the Cascadia Poetry Festival in Nanaimo, BC (April 30 to May 3, 2015). cascadiapoetryfestival.org /httpcascadiapoetryfestival-orgnews/rewilding-poetry-by-sharon-thesen/.

"My Education as a Poet." *Cordite Poetry Review* 48, no. 1 (December 2014). cordite .org.au/poetry/ohcanada/my-education-as-a-poet/.

"Earthshine: Sharon Thesen Remembers Robin Blaser." *Brick* 84 (2010).

Introduction to *North of California St.*, by George Stanley. Vancouver: New Star Books, 2014.

"Reading as Self-Help." *Reading Writers Reading: Canadian Authors' Reflections.* Edited by Danielle Schaub. Edmonton: University of Alberta Press, 2006.

"Language, Literature, and the Destruction of Cities." *Dooney's Café.* dooneyscafe .com/literature-language-destruction-cities. March 2004.

"On the H Orizon: bpNichol after Ten." *Sulfur: A Literary Biannual of the Whole Art* 44 (1999).

"Earth's Dark Anvil: Poetry of Pat Lowther." *Vancouver Review*, Fall 1997.

With Ralph Maud. "Charles Olson and Frances Boldereff: Who Will Bring It Up, My Lute? The First Letters of the Correspondence." *Sulfur: Literary Biannual of the Whole Art* 31 (1992).

"Writing the Continuing Story: Gladys Hindmarch's *The Watery Part of the World*." *Beyond Tish: New Writing, Interviews, Critical Essays*. Edited by Douglas Barbour. *West Coast Line* 25, no. 1 (Spring 1991).

"Why Women Won't Write," *Vancouver Review*, Spring 1991.

"The Turn to Formalism: Poetry and Its Discontents." *Vancouver Review*, July 1990.

"Poetry and the Dilemma of Expression." *A Mazing Space: Women Writers Writing.* Edited by Smaro Kamboureli and Shirley Neumann. Edmonton: Longspoon, 1987.

"A Few Notes on Poetry." *Poetry Canada Review*, July 1986.

"Chains of Grace: The Poetry of George Stanley." *Essays on Canadian Writing* 32 (1986).

"Who to Feel Sorry For: Teaching 'Aquarius.'" *Room of One's Own: A Feminist Journal of Literature and Criticism* 10, nos. 3–4 (1986).

"In the Song of the Alphabet: Sorrentino's Splendide-Hotel." *Review of Contemporary Fiction* 1, no. 1 (1982).

Introduction to *The Vision Tree: Selected Poems of Phyllis Webb*, by Phyllis Webb. Vancouver: Talonbooks, 1982.

PODCASTS

Thesen, Sharon, guest contributor. "Challenging, Beautiful Bioregion." *Listening to Fire Knowledges in and around the Okanagan Valley*, podcast. Judith Burr, Interdisciplinary Graduate Studies, University of British Columbia's Okanagan Campus. July 20, 2022. listeningtofirepodcast.ca/items/show/8.

Thesen, Sharon, guest. "Only the Imagination Carries Forward." *SoundBox Signals*, podcast. Karis Shearer and Nour Sallam, Simplecast. March 9, 2020. soundbox-signals.simplecast.com/episodes/only-the-imagination -carries-forward.

FILMS

Hannah Calder and Curis Emre, dirs. *Why We Write: Poets of Vernon*. 2020. theorangelamphousestudio.com/why-we-write.

SELECTED CRITICAL WORKS ON SHARON THESEN

Thiessen, Amy. "Sharon Thesen's 'The Fire.'" Honours thesis, University of British Columbia's Okanagan Campus, 2020. sharonthesenthefire.omeka.net/.

Morse, Gary Thomas. "Geomantic Riposte: 'Oyama Pink Shale.'" *Jacket2*, April 27, 2014. jacket2.org/commentary/geomantic-riposte-oyama-pink-shale.

Penberthy, Jenny, ed. "The Sharon Thesen Issue." *The Capilano Review* 3, no. 5 (Spring 2008). journals.sfu.ca/capreview/index.php/capreview/issue /view/124/63.

Thesen, Sharon. "'masquerading as simple description': A Conversation with Sharon Thesen." By Daphne Marlatt. *The Capilano Review* 3, no. 5 (Spring 2008). thecapilanoreview.com/interview-with-sharon-thesen/.

Humphreys, Helen. "In Conversation with Sharon Thesen." *Where the Words Come From: Canadian Poets in Conversation*. Edited by Tim Bowling. Gibsons, BC: Nightwood Editions, 2002.

Thesen, Sharon. "An Interview with Sharon Thesen." By Garry Thomas Morse. Sage Hill Writing. N.d. www.sagehillwriting.ca/an-interview-with-sharon -thesen.

THESEN ARCHIVES

Fonds MSG 935 – Sharon Thesen fonds, 1961–1989, McGill University Archival Collections, housed at the McGill Library, Rare Books and Special Collections (Montréal). archivalcollections.library.mcgill.ca/index.php /sharon-thesen-fonds.

Fonds MsC-33 – Sharon Thesen fonds at Simon Fraser University Special Collections and Books (Burnaby, BC). Undated but from 1960s to 1990s. atom.archives.sfu.ca/msc-33.

Index of Titles and First Lines

Italicized text denotes first lines, text in SMALL CAPS denotes poem titles, and regular text denotes titled subsections of poems. In poems with untitled subsections, numbered or not, only the first line of the first section is included.

A dove-grey morning 109

A HOLY EXPERIMENT 201

A PAIR OF SCISSORS 12

Adults 57

AFTER ROY KIYOOKA'S FUNERAL 3

After Spicer 95

Ahhhh … 49

An array of hairnets – the hairnets of
   Jove's wife 206

An autumn 79

An open space signals 55

Apparently sane 58

Appearances are everything. 96

Are dim. Are a missing 65

AT MY MOTHER'S IN PRINCE
   GEORGE 223

Axe Murderer 50

BEING ADULTS 55

Being adults 57

BIOGRAPHY OF A WOMAN 31

CLEMATIS MONTANA RUBENS 85

CONFABULATIONS 107

Contretemps 52

Do not read these words. 92

Echolocation 98

Expressways and turnpikes, off-ramps,
   antacid vapour lights. 205

FIVE PRELUDES 7

For this ailment, for that, he had
   a cure. 203

FROM TOLEDO 79

GALA ROSES 69

Gaunt hills 217

He could have been a soldier 203

How long 90

I DRIVE THE CAR 99

I drive the car 99

I take a kitchen chair out to the front porch 3

If it's not flowing I'll not tell 69

In small rivers 53

IN THE CAR WASH 231

In the car wash 231

In the Fashion Tress beauty salon 35

In worn-out chairs, we sat in his
   kitchen. 202

Jerry Geiger was Boldereff's friend in
   Woodward, Pennsylvania, many years
   ago. 201

Last night my young friend and I 56

Look at that mountain. That must be Shasta
   Mountain. 91

Look out! 50

Love, 94

Magic 96

Making a Break 55

Mars glared 143

My son asks me 98

New Year's 58

Now only the imagination 184

OH, HELLO COUNT, HOW ARE YOU,
   DO COME IN 197

On the way 52

One night, her friend Jerry had her look at the
   sky through his telescope. 201

Out the window 93

PARTS OF SPEECH 89

Person Place or Thing 93

RADIO NEW FRANCE RADIO 184

Responsive 51

Rosary 53

Rows and jars of homemade reddish-
   brown & 202

Saved 56

She flew, she was up 103

She was so intelligent 31

SIX 49

SKYLARKS 139

Someone about to go back to the hotel room 7

Summer 54

Sunday painters, these 49

The 89

The Argument Begins with A 94

THE BEGINNING OF THE LONG
   DASH 35

THE CELEBRATION 169

The clock said 10 to 3. 61

THE CONSUMPTIVES AT TRANQUILLE
   SANATORIUM, 1953 217

The crossings 89

THE FIRE 143

THE GOOD BACTERIA 154

The house is built 54

The imaginative 95

THE NETS OF BEING 206

THE OCCASIONS 65

THE PARROT 103

The river runs by so quietly 223

The Susquehanna would reveal 205

The time and the car have to go. The light has
   to fall 197

THE WATERMELON 61

The willow tree in winter, 173

They had a view of the twinkling city as
   they ate. 154

This & That 91

Through the blue 139

To be bold in my own way, 12

To See 90

Usage 92

Was it a poorly attended event, a
   celebration 169

We were staying at an old, old inn. 204

WEEPING WILLOW 173

What if something supernatural
   happened? 204

While asleep I dreamed the world had
   changed. 85

You can do it the easy way 51

Erín Moure has published over fifty books: poetry, essays, memoir, as well as translations and co-translations of poetry from French, Spanish, Galician, Portuguese, Portuñol, and Ukrainian (with Roman Ivashkiv) into English. Recent works are *Planetary Noise: Selected Poetry of Erín Moure* (Wesleyan University Press, 2017), *Sitting Shiva on Minto Avenue, by Toots* (New Star Books, 2017), Wilson Bueno's *Paraguayan Sea* (Nightboat, 2017), Uxío Novoneyra's *The Uplands: Book of the Courel and Other Poems* (Veliz Books, 2020), Juan Gelman's *Sleepless Nights under Capitalism* (Eulalia Books, 2020), Chantal Neveu's *This Radiant Life* (Book*hug Press, 2020), and Chus Pato's *The Face of the Quartzes* (Veliz Books, 2021). She lives in Montréal.

Poet, editor, and teacher **Sharon Thesen** has spent almost all her life in British Columbia. *Artemis Hates Romance,* her first book of poetry (Coach House Press, 1980), was followed by eleven more, three of them finalists for the Governor General's Award for Poetry: *Confabulations* (Oolichan Books, 1984); *The Beginning of the Long Dash* (Coach House Press, 1987), and *The Good Bacteria* (House of Anansi Press, 2006). She edited *The Vision Tree: Selected Poems of Phyllis Webb* (Talonbooks, 1982), which won the Governor General's Award for Poetry, two editions of *The New Long Poem Anthology* (House of Anansi, 1991, and Talonbooks, 2001), and, with Ralph Maud, two volumes of correspondence between American poet Charles Olson and book-designer and Joyce scholar Frances Boldereff (Weslyan University Press, 1999, and Talonbooks, 2012). *The Receiver* (New Star Books, 2017) and *The Wig-Maker* (with Janet Gallant, New Star Books, 2021) are her most recent collections. She lives in BC's Lake Country. In 2020, UBC Okanagan honoured Thesen's writing, editing, and teaching career with the creation of the Sharon Thesen Lecture, an annual talk in creative writing by an invited writer.